1 MONTH OF
FREE
READING

at

www.ForgottenBooks.com

By purchasing this book you are eligible for one month membership to ForgottenBooks.com, giving you unlimited access to our entire collection of over 1,000,000 titles via our web site and mobile apps.

To claim your free month visit: www.forgottenbooks.com/free149586

ISBN 978-0-483-32935-5
PIBN 10149586

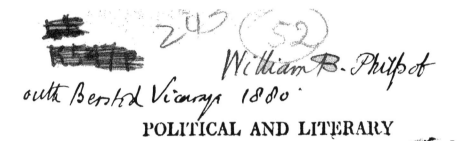

POLITICAL AND LITERARY

ANECDOTES

OF

HIS OWN TIMES.

BY DR. WILLIAM KING,

PRINCIPAL OF ST. MARY HALL, OXON.

SECOND EDITION.

But lo! at once the pealing concerts cease,
And crowded theatres are hush'd in peace.
See, on yon sage how all attentive stand,
To catch his darting eye, and waving hand.
Hark! he begins, with all a Tully's art,
To pour the dictates of a Cato's heart:
Skill'd to pronounce what noblest thoughts inspire,
He blends the speaker's with the patriot's fire;
Bold to conceive, nor timorous to conceal,
What Britons dare to think, he dares to tell.
'Tis his alike the ear and eye to charm,
To win with action, and with sense to warm;
Untaught in flowery periods to dispense
The lulling sounds of sweet impertinence:
In frowns or smiles he gains an equal prize,
Nor meanly fears to fall, nor creeps to rise.

T. WARTON.

ADVERTISEMENT.

A FRIEND, who was a long time a prisoner in France, met with the following work in the possession of two ladies, relatives of the writer, Dr. King. From the interesting passages which he was permitted to extract, the Editor conceived that the original might be well worthy of publication; he therefore desired his friend to procure it, and found, on a comparison of the hand-writing with that which is well ascertained to be Dr. King's in the account-books of St. Mary Hall in Oxford (of which he was many years the principal), that there is every reason to suppose this MS. to have been written by Dr. King himself. From certain minute additions and corrections of the language, there can be little doubt of its having been intended for publication. It contains a very striking character of the Pretender, and many interesting anecdotes of the jacobite party, to which he was strongly attached, and with the leaders of which he was intimately acquainted. There will also be found in it an amusing *jeu d'esprit* called the Somnium Academicum, written in very pure Latin, for which he was much distinguished; and many pleasant stories of the great men and literary characters of his days, with some elegant criticism on the Latin poets. Having said thus much on the history and contents of this publication, it will be necessary to add a short account of the writer for the instruction of those who may be ignorant of his name and character.

* " Dr. William King, son of the Rev. Peregrine King, was born at Stepney,

* From Chalmers's Biography.

in Middlesex, in 1685; and, after a
school-education at Salisbury, was entered of Baliol College, Oxford; July 9;
1701. Proceeding ion the law line, he
took his doctor's degree in 1715; was
secretary to the Duke of Ormond and
the Earl of Arran, when chancellors of
the university; and was made Principal
of St. Mary Hall in 1718. When be was
candidate for the university, in 1722, he
resigned his office of secretary; but his
other preferment he enjoyed (and it was
all he did enjoy) to the time of his death.
Dr. Clarke, who opposed him, carried
his election; and, after this disappointment, 1727, he went over to Ireland.
With what design he went thither is to
us unknown; but his enemies say, it was
for the purposes of intrigue, and to expose himself to sale. But he says himself, and there are no facts alleged to
disprove it, "at no time of my life, either
in England or Ireland, either from the

present or any former government, have I asked, or endeavoured by any means to obtain, a place, pension, or employment of any kind. I could assign many reasons for my conduct; but one answer I have always ready: I inherited a patrimony, which I found sufficient to supply all my wants, and to leave me at liberty to pursue those liberal studies which afforded me the most solid pleasures in my youth, and are the delight and enjoyment of my old age. Besides, I always conceived a secret horror of a state of servility and dependence: and I never yet saw a placeman or a courtier, whether in a higher or lower class, whether a priest or a layman, who was his own master." During his stay in Ireland, he is said to have written an epic poem, called " The Toast," bearing the name of Scheffer, a Laplander, as its author, and of Peregrine O'Donald, esq. as its translator; which was a political satire, and was printed and given away to friends, but never sold. Dr. Warton says, that the Countess of Newburgh was aimed at in this satire.

" On the dedication of Radcliffe's library, 1749, he spoke a Latin oration in the theatre at Oxford, which was received with the highest acclamations by a splendid auditory. Mr. Warton, in " The Triumphs of Isis," pays him a very great compliment on that occasion. But this oration, which was soon after printed, did not meet with such favourable reception from the public; for he was attacked in several pamphlets on account of it, in which he was charged with writing barbarous Latin, with being disaffected to the government, and that he instigated the younger members of the university to sedition and licentiousness; very heavy accusations, if we may not candidly suppose them dictated by the spirit of malevolence and party zeal. And again, in

1755, when the memorable election con-
test happened in Oxfordshire, his attachment to the old interest drew on him the
resentment of the new. He was libelled
in newspapers and in pamphlets, and
charged with the following particulars,
viz. that he was an Irishman; that
he had received subscriptions for books
never published to the amount of 1500*l.*
of which sum he had defrauded his sub-
scribers; that he had offered himself to
sale both in England and Ireland, and
was not found worth the purchase; that
he was the writer of " The London Evening Post;" the author of a book in Queen
Anne's reign, entitled " Political Considerations," 1710, in which there was
false English; and of a book then just
published, called " The Dreamer," 1754,
8vo. At this time he published his
" Apology," in 4to. and plausibly vindicated himself from the several matters
charged on him, except only the last ar-

ticle, of his being the author of " The Dreamer;" and warmly retaliated on his adversaries.

" He was the author of, 1. " Miltoni epistola ad Pollionem" (Lord Polwarth). 2. " Sermo Pedestris." 3. " Scamnum, ecloga." 4. " Templum libertatis," in three books. 5. " Tres Oratiunculæ." 6. " Epistola objurgatoria." 7. " Antonietti ducis Corscorum epistola ad Corscos de rege eligendo." 8. " Eulogium Jacci Etonensis." 9. " Aviti epistola ad Perillam, virginem Scotam," &c. 10. " Oratiuncula habita in domo convocationis Oxon. cum epistola dedicatoria," 1757, and " Epitaphium Richardi Nash." Besides these, he published the first five volumes of Dr. South's sermons.—He was known and esteemed by the first men of his time for wit and learning; and must be allowed to have been a polite scholar, an excellent orator, and an elegant and easy writer, both in Latin and English. He died Dec. 30, 1763, having sketched his own character in an elegant epitaph, in which, while he acknowledges his failings, he claims the praise of benevolence, temperance, and fortitude. This epitaph was to be engraved on a silver case, in which he directed his heart should be preserved in some convenient part of St. Mary Hall. He was buried in Ealing church, but the inscription is on a marble tablet in the chapel of St. Mary Hall. There is a striking likeness of Dr. King in Worlidge's view of the installation of Lord Westmorland as chancellor of Oxford, in 1761."

PREFACE.

I AM now in my seventy-sixth year, and am often confined by the infirmities which are incident to old age. In some of those hours the following work hath been a part of my amusement; I may properly call it an amusement, because it required no study, nor any continued application; for, as it consists of detached pieces, a kind of table-talk, I could therefore lay it aside and return to it when I pleased. Most of the anec-

dotes which I have inserted are
from my own knowledge; the rest
were related to me by those friends
on whose honour and veracity I can
depend.   As to the observations
which I have made on human life,
the reflections on men and manners,
and, the remarks on books and authors, they are my present sentiments, which I have delivered with
an honest freedom, without pretend-
ing, however, to control the judgment or opinion of any other person.

ANECDOTES, &c.

ÆQUANIMITY, or the *æquus animus* of HORACE, which is neither elated by prosperity, nor depressed by any adverse fortune, is constitutional, and not to be acquired by philosophy or religion.

I am likewise of opinion, that what we call HUMAN PRUDENCE is born with us; though I confess, it may be greatly assisted and improved by experience and observation.

A benevolent man, endowed with human prudence and with that equality of

B

mind I have before mentioned, consti-
tutes his own happiness, conciliates the
affection of all about him, and may always be the most useful member in any
society. But a man, in whom these qualities are united, is scarce to be found
amongst half a million : and in the course
of a long life I cannot recollect more
than one or two examples.

I have an equal mind, and generally
very good spirits; and, if I do not mis-
take myself, I have a good heart : but I
have a very small portion of human prudence. And for want of this excellent
quality, I have twice in my life lost the
opportunity of acquiring a very large
fortune in the most irreproachable manner. It has been owing to the same defect that my patrimony hath been so ill

managed, and so much impaired. I have run myself into many inconveniences. I have made enemies when I did not intend to give the least offence, and I have suffered much by family misfortunes; all which a little human sagacity and foresight would easily have prevented. However let me be ever, thankful to Divine Providence, that I have never wanted the necessaries, nor even the comforts of life: and what, has given me a very singular pleasure, I have always been able to spare something to assist a poor friend.

THE KING OF ARRAGON made a very good judgment of human life when he said, There were only four things in the world worth living for, OLD WINE TO

DRINK, OLD WOOD TO BURN, OLD BOOKS
TO READ, and OLD FRIENDS TO CONVERSE
WITH. And a greater king than ALPHON-
SUS, after having enjoyed all the pleasures and the utmost felicity this world
was capable of providing for him, pronounced the whole to be VANITY. I
have asked many of my acquaintance
this question, Whether, if a power of
living their lives over again were granted
to them, they would accept it? and I
never heard one man of sense answer in
the affirmative. Select a person, who,
according to the estimate of human happiness, is the happiest of all mortals,
who in appearance is possessed of every
thing that can satisfy his senses or gratify his passions, I will venture to affirm,
that he is in pursuit of something, which

is at a great distance from him, and when he has obtained it, he will want something else, which perhaps he never can obtain. But if his good fortune should reach this last something, which is to complete his felicity, then ask him again if he would be willing to go back to his infancy, and act the very same parts in life a second time; and I much doubt whether he would undertake the labour, although he were to be rewarded at the end of it with Mahomet's paradise*.

* Since I wrote this, I perceive that the learned M. *Maupertuis* hath confirmed my opinion. *Who*, says he, *would choose to live his life over again, and to pass through the same individual scenes?* The author of a book published last year, entitled VARIOUS PROSPECTS of MANKIND, NATURE, and PROVIDENCE, endeavours to answer this question and confute M. MAUPERTUIS's proposition. His answer is ingenious, but very unsatisfactory. He reasons from

I HOPE that I shall not offend ortho-
doxy, as it is not inconsistent with the
religion which I profess, if I assert, that
this world is a place of punishment, as
well as a place of trial; which is a proposition, I think, that will almost admit
of a mathematical demonstration.

'A PRESENCE OF MIND is a very rare,
but a very happy and useful talent, and
is a certain guard against many mischiefs
and inconveniences, to which human life
is continually exposed. It is something
very different from impudence, or a
vain assurance. A PRESENCE of MIND
is always well-bred, and is generally

data which cannot be allowed him. A better argument than any he hath used would have been to
assure his readers, That he himself would be glad
to live his life over again.

accompanied with wit and courage. Amongst all my acquaintance I cannot recollect more than three persons who were eminently possessed of this quality, Dr. ATTERBURY, Bishop of *Rochester*, the *Earl* of STAIRS, who was our ambassador in *France* the beginning of the last reign, and Dr. JAMES MONRO, who was many years physician of *Bethlem* hospital.

In 1715 I dined with the DUKE of ORMONDE at Richmond. We were fourteen at table. There was my Lord MARR, my Lord JERSEY, my Lord ARRAN, my Lord LANDSDOWN, Sir WILLIAM WYNDHAM, Sir REDMOND EVERARD, and ATTERBURY, Bishop of *Rochester*. The rest of the company I do not exactly remember. During the dinner there was a jocular dispute (I forget how it was introduced) concerning short prayers. Sir WILLIAM WYNDHAM told us, that the shortest prayer he had ever heard was the prayer of a common soldier just before the battle of *Blenheim,* ' *O God, if there be a God, save my soul, if I have a soul!'.* This was followed by a general laugh. I immediately reflected that such a treatment of the subject was too ludicrous, at least very improper, where a learned and religious prelate was one of the company. But I had soon an opportunity of making a different reflection. ATTERBURY, seeming to join in the conversation, and applying himself to Sir WILLIAM WYNDHAM, said "Your prayer, Sir WILLIAM, is indeed very short: but I remember another as short, but a much better, offered up likewise by a poor soldier in the same circumstances, ' *O God, if in the day of battle I forget thee, do thou not forget me!* '" This, as ATTER-BURY pronounced it with his usual grace and dignity, was a very gentle and polite reproof, and was immediately felt by the whole company. And the Duke of OR-MONDE, who was the best bred man of his age, suddenly turned the discourse to another subject.

CARDINAL POLIGNAC, the author of the *Anti Lucretius*, was a fine gentleman, as well as an elegant and polite scholar. He had a most engaging affability, and a peculiar art and manner of obliging every man, who was introduced to him, to lay aside all restraint. I had not been with him a quarter of an hour, when I found myself as easy as if I had been educated in his family. We had some talk of his *Anti Lucretius*, and I took that opportunity of complimenting. him upon a small specimen of that work, which had been published in the *Bibliotheque Choisis*, or some other of the literary journals.. " That specimen,". said the Cardinal, . ". which you have. read, was published by Monsieur Le Clerc. He importuned me for a sight of my MS. which I refused him, as I had always resolved that this poem should not appear till after my death. However, to gratify Le Clerc's curiosity, I repeated to him those verses (about 150), which he hath published. I repeated them once only; and yet he was able to carry

them away in his memory, although·he
was then seventy years old." I should
have inclined to believe that the Cardinal had been deceived, and that LE
CLERC had by some means got at the
MS. if I had not known in my own family a most amazing instance of the
strength of memory.

The Cardinal observing that during
dinner I drank only water, and being
told I never drank any other liquor,
said, turning to me, " Whilst I was ambassador at *Rome*, and since my return
to *France*, I have entertained more than
five hundred of your countrymen, and
you are the only water-drinker I have
found in the whole number." This was
in September 1737. There is an excellent print of the Cardinal, engraved by
Chereau, from a picture of ——.

A MAN, who has contracted the pernicious habit of drinking drams, is conscious that he is taking in a slow poison, and therefore he will never own it either to his friend or his physician, though it is visible to all his acquaintance. POPE and I, with my Lord ORRERY and Sir HARRY BEDINGFIELD, dined with the late Earl of BURLINGTON. After the first course POPE grew sick, and went out of the room. When dinner was ended, and the cloth removed, my Lord BURLINGTON said he would go out, and see what was become of POPE. And soon after they returned together. But POPE, who had been casting up his dinner, looked very pale, and complained much. My Lord asked him if he would have some mulled wine or a glass of old sack, which POPE refused. I told my

Lord BURLINGTON that he wanted a dram. Upon which the little man expressed some resentment against me, and said he would not taste any spirits, and that he abhorred drams as much as I did. However I persisted, and assured my Lord BURLINGTON that he could not oblige our friend more at that instant than by ordering a large glass of cherry-brandy to be set before him. This was done, and in less than half an hour, while my Lord was acquainting us with an affair which engaged our attention, POPE had sipped up all the brandy. POPE's frame of body did not promise long life; but he certainly hastened his death by feeding much on high-seasoned dishes, and drinking spirits.

A PRESBYTERIAN teacher, or one, designed for the office, though he changes his condition, and has an opportunity of conversing with the politest men in the kingdom, yet he will always retain his original cant. CHANDLER, the popish Bishop of *London,* and SECKER, Bishop of *Oxford,* are both converts from presbytery. They are frequent preachers; but the cant of their education renders their discourses very disagreeable to a good ear. Their parts are moderate, and nearly equal; but their characters are very different. CHANDLER is a real convert, and as void of all hypocrisy as he is free from pride and ambition.

PRAISE is the strongest satire, and the most pleasing: but it requires great art and judgment to manage and conduct an irony. I once said, talking on this subject with Dr. SWIFT, that the Rhapsody was the best satire he had ever composed. He assured me that immediately after this poem was published, he received a message of thanks from the whole . * * * * * *. This I can easily conceive, as irony is not a figure in the German Rhetoric. If Mr. POPE in the place, where he calls Lord COB-HAM a coward, had complimented a German Colonel with the same appellation, my little friend, I fear, would have fared very ill——The Rhapsody would probably have continued to Dr. SWIFT the favour which it had acquired him, if Lord HARVEY had not undeceived Q. C. and taken some pains to teach her the use and power of the irony.

THE last time I dined with Dean SWIFT, which was about three years before he fell into that distemper which totally deprived him of his understanding, I observed, that he was affected by the wine which he drank, about a pint of claret. The next morning, as we were walking together in his garden, he complained much of his head, when I took the liberty to tell him (for I most sincerely loved him) that I was afraid he drank too much wine. He was a little startled, and answered, " that as to his drinking he had always looked on himself as a very temperate man; for he never exceeded the quantity which his physician had allowed and prescribed him." Now his physician never drank less than two bottles of claret after his dinner.

THE EARL OF CHESTERFIELD, who some years ago resigned his employment of Secretary of State, because he would not submit to be a cypher in his office, and work under a man who had not an hundredth part of his knowledge and understanding, resolved to meddle no more in public affairs. However he was lately so much disgusted with our bad measures, that he could not help animadverting on them, though in his usual calm and polite manner. His petition to the King is an excellent satire, and hath discovered to the whole nation how, at a time when we are oppressed with taxes, and the common people every where grown mutinous for want of bread, the public money is squandered away in pensions, generally bestowed upon the most worthless men. I fancy it was this witty petition which furnished the Irish parliament with the hint of forming so many honest resolutions concerning the great number of pensions, with which that kingdom is loaded.

We are never grieved when a man of merit, or any one, who has done the least service to his country, is rewarded out of the public treasure: but we cannot without great indignation behold a sum of money sufficient to maintain a large hospital given annually to one great Lord to support his luxury, and to another to gratify his avarice. I am well assured that the present D. of D. has received more than two hundred thousand pounds in places and pensions since the accession of King GEORGE I.,

and yet it would be difficult to prove
that this man had ever done any service
or honour either to his country or his
benefactor. Upon reading my Lord
CHESTERFIELD's petition, I sent him this
compliment:

Quæ venit è coelo monitoris epistola PHOEBI,
   Dicimus hanc satiram, culte PHILIPPE, tuam.
Ille etiam PHOEBO fortasse simillimus esset,
   Qui rex indignis munera nulla daret.

WHO amongst all the modern writers
is to be more esteemed and admired
than Monsieur FENELON, Archbishop of
Cambray, and author of *Telemachus;*
whose piety, politeness and humanity,
were equal to his great learning? RAM-
SAY, the author of *Cyrus*, who was educated in Monsieur FENELON's family,
acquainted me with an anecdote, which

hath ever made me reverence the memory of this excellent man. Some *German* officers, who were prisoners at *Cambray*, were invited to dine with the Archbishop, whose table was always open to the officers of the *French* Garrison, of which a certain number dined with him every day. The *Germans* during the dinner were continually calling for bumpers of wine. The *French* seemed to sneer at this behaviour of the *German* officers, and looked on them with a kind of contempt: which Monsieur FENELON observing, called for an half-pint glass of Burgundy, (which perhaps was more than he had ever taken at one meal before), and drank it off to the health of the prisoners. This was a handsome compliment to the *Germans*, and a proper reprimand to his own countrymen. But as soon as the *German* officers were gone, he thus admonished the *French* gentlemen. "You should endeavour to divest yourselves of all national prejudices, and never condemn the customs and manners of a foreign people, because they are altogether different from your own. I am a true *French*-man, and love my country; but I love mankind better than my country."

THE DUKE OF ORLEANS, who was regent of *France* during the minority of the present King LEWIS the XVth, was most debauched in his life and abandoned in his morals. And yet he appeared to be a prince of great humanity, and a lover of public justice. When Count HORN was sentenced to be broke on the wheel, Duke D'AREMBERG, and the whole family of HORN, applied to the Regent for a pardon. But not succeeding in this attempt, and finding the Regent inflexible, they requested that the Count's sentence might only be changed, and to avoid an ignominious death, which would be a lasting stain in the whole family, that he might have the favour of being beheaded. But this likewise the Regent refused, and made this answer: " Count HORN is my relation as well as yours : but the infamy is not in the punishment, but in the crime." When the Prince of * * * * solicited the Regent to pardon a murder, which he had committed, after having been pardoned for the same crime once or twice before; " I will pardon you," says the Regent, " but take notice and keep this in your memory, I will certainly pardon the man, whoever he be, that kills you." This monitory had a proper effect, and put a stop to the barbarities of this *Bourbon* Prince, who presumed that his quality of Prince of the blood was a licence for murder. These two answers of the Regent of *France* deserve to be written in letters of gold.

MOST OF THE COMMENTATORS on the *Greek* and *Roman* poets think it sufficient to explain their author, and to give us the various readings. Some few indeed have made us remark the excellency of the poet's plan, the elegance of his diction, and the propriety of his thoughts, at the same time pointing out as examples the most striking and beautiful descriptions. RUÆUS in his comment on VIRGIL certainly excelled all his fellow-labourers, who were appointed to explain and publish a series of the *Roman* classics for the use of the DAUPHIN. His mythological, historical, and geographical notes are a great proof of his learning and diligence. But he hath not entered into the spirit of the author, and displayed the great art and judgment of the poet, particularly his knowledge of men and manners. The learned Jesuit perhaps imagined that remarks of this sort were foreign to the employment of a commentator, or for some political reasons he might think proper to omit them. And yet, in my opinion, nothing could have been more instructive and entertain⸗

ing, as his comment was chiefly designed for the use of a young prince. The *Æneid* furnishes us with many examples to the purpose I mention. However, that I may be the better understood, the following remark will explain my meaning. In the beginning of the first book *Juno* makes a visit to *Æolus*, and desires him to raise a storm and destroy the *Trojan* fleet, because she hated the whole nation on account of the judgment of *Paris*, or, as she was pleased to express herself, because the *Trojans* were her enemies. *Gens inimica mihi*, &c. *Juno* was conscious that she asked a god to oblige her by an act which was both unjust and cruel, and therefore she accompanied her request with the offer of *Deiopeia*, the most beautiful nymph in her train: a

powerful bribe, and such as she imagined
Æolus could not resist. She was not
disappointed : *Æolus* accepted her offer,
and executed her commands as far as he
was able. What I have to observe here,
in the first place, is the necessity of that
short speech, in which *Juno* addresses
herself to *Æolus*. She had no time to
lose. The *Trojan* fleet was in the *Tus-
can* sea, sailing with a fair wind, and
in a few hours would probably have
been in a safe harbour. *Æolus* therefore answered in as few words as the
goddess had addressed herself to him.
But his answer is very curious. He
takes no notice of the offer of *Deiopeia*,
for whom upon any other occasion he
would have thanked *Juno* upon his knees.
But now, when she was given, and ac-

cepted by him as a bribe, and as the wages of cruelty and injustice, he endeavoured by his answer to avoid that imputation, and pretended he had such a grateful sense of the favours which *Juno* had formerly conferred on him, when she introduced him to *Jupiter*'s table, that it was his duty to obey her commands on all occasions:

Tuus; O Regina, quod optes,
Explorare labor; mihi jussa capessere fas est.

And thus insinuated even to *Juno* herself, that this was the sole motive of his ready compliance with her request. I am here put in mind of something similar, which happened in Sir ROBERT WALPOLE's administration. He wanted to carry a question in the House of Commons, to which he knew there would be great opposition, and which was disliked by some of his own dependents. As he was passing through the Court of Requests, he met a member of the contrary party, whose avarice he imagined would not reject a large bribe. He took him aside, and said, " Such a question comes on this day; give me your vote, and here is a bank bill of 2000*l.*," which he put into his hands. The member made him this answer. " Sir ROBERT, you have lately served some of my particular friends; and when my wife was last at court, the King was very gracious to her, which must have happened at your instance. I should therefore think myself very ungrateful (*putting the bank bill into his pocket*) if I were to refuse the favour you are now pleased to ask

me." This incident, if wrought up by
a man of humour, would make a pleasant
scene in a political farce. But to return
to *Virgil*. The short conference between
Juno and *Æolus* is a sufficient proof of
the poet's excellent judgment. It de-
monstrates his knowledge of the world,
and more particularly his acquaintance
with the customs and manners of a great
prince's court. Hence we may learn that
a bribe, if it be large enough, and sea-
sonably offered, will frequently overcome
the virtue and resolution of persons of
the highest rank, and that the power of
love and beauty will sometimes corrupt
a god, and compel him to discover a
weakness unworthy of a man.

I HAVE, A VENERATION for VIRGIL:

I admire HORACE: but I love OVID.
The *Georgics* is perhaps the most finished
poem of all which are now extant in any
language. The Odes of HORACE are a
master-piece, and beautiful beyond description: where he has imitated *Pindar*
(which he has done, I think, but once in
the beginning of that ode *Quem virum
aut Heroa,* &c.) he has evidently excelled him. But neither of these great
poets knew how to move the passions so
well as OVID; witness some of the tales
of his Metamorphoses, particularly the
story of *Ceyx* and *Halcyone,* which I
never read without weeping. The *Medea*
of OVID is a great loss. I persuade myself if this work, which all the ancients
have so highly commended, was now extant, it would bear the palm from all our

modern tragedies, whether *French* or *English*. No judicious critic hath ever yet denied that OVID has more wit than any other poet of the *Augustan* age. That he has too much, and that his fancy is too luxuriant, is the fault generally imputed to him. This he would probably have corrected, if he had had the liberty of reviewing his *Metamorphoses:*

Emendaturus, si licuisset, erat.

But, methinks, I am much better pleased that this did not happen, since by varying, and expressing the same thought in a different manner, this poet hath left us a standing proof of the copiousness and elegance of the *Latin* tongue. This is of great use to our youth in learning *Latin*, and indeed to all who attempt to write in that lan-

guage. What would I give for the chip-
pings of the *Æneid?* For we are told
that *Tucca* and *Varius* cut off from that
poem as much as they left, before it
was offered to the public. All the im-
perfections of *Ovid* are really pleasing.
But who would not excuse all his faults
on account of his many excellencies,
particularly his descriptions, which have
never been equalled?

COURAGE, in which I include a fortitude of mind as well as personal bra-
very, should not be wanting in any person who is engaged in the public service,
whether he be in a civil or military station, or who has formed a design of acquiring either. Without courage a man
of the greatest abilities and integrity will

scarce be able to preserve his character, and in some exigencies to save his person. His prudence will frequently be confounded, and his honesty will be warped by his fears. The late Lord BOLEN-BROKE, so well known by his writings, executed his employment of Secretary of State with great address and sufficiency. When after Queen ANNE's death he was impeached of high treason, Sir THOMAS HARE, his under secretary, secreted all the papers of any consequence, before the office was searched. But my Lord BOLENBROKE, after thanking Sir THOMAS HARE and acknowledging the greatest obligations to him, as to one who had preserved him, was induced either by the fair promises or the menaces of Mr. STANHOPE *, to resign all these papers

* See Parke's Preface to Bolingbroke's Letters. ı

into the hands of the secret committee, and thus furnished them with materials whereon to ground all the articles of his impeachment. If Lord BOLENBROKE had had the firmness and resolution of the EARL of OXFORD, he would not have been forced into banishment, and been deprived of his estate and honours.

THE late DUKE of WHARTON had very bright parts, a great vivacity, a quick apprehension, a ready wit and a natural eloquence, and all improved by an excellent education. I do not believe that any young nobleman, on his first entrance into the House of Lords, hath appeared with such advantage. His speech in defence of Dr. ATTERBURY, Bishop of *Rochester*, was heard with universal applause and admiration, and was indeed not unworthy of the oldest and most accomplished senator, or the most able and eloquent lawyer in either House of Parliament. So that he might have promised himself the first employments in the kingdom : and he had no small share of ambition. But he defeated his own designs. He had no prudence or economy ; and he wanted personal courage. The last however would probably have been concealed, if he had been a sober man. But he drank immoderately, and was very abusive, and sometimes very mischievous in his wine ; so that he drew on himself frequent challenges, which he would never answer. On other accounts, likewise, his character was become very prostitute. So that having lost his honour, he left his country.

SINCE the beginning of the present war, Admiral BING was condemned to death by one court-martial, and my Lord GEORGE SACKVILLE was disgraced by another. But both were acquitted of the crime of cowardice. And yet this is the only charge brought against them both before and since their trials, by the voice of the people. If I were compelled to deliver my own opinion, I should think myself better justified in adding my vote to the cry of the multitude, than concurring in the sentence of either of the court-martials.

COLONEL CECIL, who was agent for the CHEVALIER ST. GEORGE, and succeeded my Lord ORRERY, the father of the present Earl of CORKE, in that office, had a weak judgment, and was very illiterate, and in many other respects was wholly unqualified for such a delicate commission. I believe he was a man of honour, and yet he betrayed his master. For he suffered himself to be cajoled and duped by Sir ROBERT WALPOLE to such a degree, as to be fully persuaded that Sir ROBERT had formed a design to restore the House of STUART. For this reason he communicated to Sir ROBERT all his despatches, and there was not a scheme which the CHEVALIER's court or the jacobites in *England* had projected during Sir ROBERT's long administration, of which that minister was not early informed, and was therefore able to defeat it without any noise or expense. The DUCHESS of BUCKINGHAM, who was closely connected with CECIL, had made two or three journeys to *Versailles* in order to persuade CARDINAL FLEURY. But she got nothing from the CARDINAL but compliments and civil excuses, and was laught at by both courts for her pompous manner of travelling, in which she affected the state of a sovereign prince. It is no wonder that this woman, who was half-mad, was induced by CECIL to entertain the same favourable opinion with himself of Sir ROBERT WALPOLE, and consequently all the letters and instructions which she received from *Rome* were without reserve communicated to him. He was at last so much in her good graces, that she offered to marry him, which Sir ROBERT very civilly declined. However, to testify her good opinion of him, she appointed him one of her executors. After Sir ROBERT WALPOLE's resignation, the new ministry ordered CECIL, whose agency was well known, to be taken into custody, which gave Sir ROBERT the occasion of saying to some of his friends, that the government had taken up the man from whom he had received all his information of the jacobite measures.

IT IS CERTAIN, that all our national misfortunes since the accession of the House of HANOVER must be chiefly ascribed to WALPOLE's administration. He unhinged all the principles and morals of our people, and changed the government into a system of corruption. He openly ridiculed virtue and merit, and promoted no man to any employ-

ment of profit or honour, who had scru-
ples of conscience, or refused implicitly
to obey his commands. He was a ready
speaker, understood the business of parliament, and knew how to manage an
House of Commons, which however was
not a very difficult task, if it be considered
that a majority of the members were of
his own nomination. He seemed to have
great resolution; and yet he was once
so much intimidated by the clamours
of the people without doors, that he
thought it expedient to give up one of
his most favourite schemes. He had
besides' some difficulties to encounter
through his whole administration, which
were not known to the public. A friend
of mine who dined with him one day
téte-à-téte took occasion to compliment

him , on the great 'honour and power
which he enjoyed as prime minister.
" Doctor," says he, " I have great power,
it is true: but I have two cursed draw-
backs, *Hanover*, and the * * * avarice."
This minister, who thought he had established himself beyond a possibility of
being shaken, fell at last by his too
great security: if he may be said to fall,
who went out of employment with an
Earldom and a pension of 4000*l.* or
5000*l.* a year.

Some very worthy gentlemen and true
lovers of their country were inclined to
pray for the continuance of Sir ROBERT's
ministry, as the old woman prayed for
the life of *Dionysius* the tyrant. They
judged that his successors would be
worse ministers, and worse men; that

they would pursue his measures without his abilities: and the event has verified their prediction.

No INCIDENT in this reign astonished us so much as the conduct of my Lord BATH, who chose to receive his honours as the wages of iniquity, which he might have had as the reward of virtue. By his opposition to a mal-administration for near twenty years, he had contracted an universal esteem, and was considered as the chief bulwark and protector of the *British* liberties. By the fall of WALPOLE, he enjoyed for some days a kind of sovereign power. During this interval, it was expected that he would have formed a patriot ministry, and have put the public affairs in such a train as would necessarily, in a very short time, have repaired all the breaches in our constitution. But how were we deceived! He deserted the cause of his country: he betrayed his friends and adherents: he ruined his character; and from a most glorious eminence sunk down to a degree of contempt. The first time Sir ROBERT (who was now EARL of ORFORD) met him in the House of Lords, he threw out this reproach: " My Lord BATH, you and I are now two as insignificant men as any in *England*." In which he spoke the truth of my Lord BATH, but not of himself. For my Lord ORFORD was consulted by the ministers to the last day of his life.

Mr. W. LEVISON, my Lord GOWER's brother, told me that he happened to be in the House of Lords, and standing next Sir ROBERT WALPOLE, when there was a warm debate concerning some ministerial measures. In the midst of the debate says Sir ROBERT to him; "You see with what zeal and vehemence these gentlemen oppose, and yet I know the price of every man in this House except three, and your brother is one of them." Sir ROBERT was frequently very unguarded in his expressions: for nothing certainly could have been thrown out more injurious to the honour of the House of Lords. Besides, this was an open confession of his manner of governing, and to what a great height he had carried corruption.

Sir ROBERT lived long enough to

know that my Lord GOWER had his price as well as the rest, and was unworthy of forming his triumvirate.

My LORD GOWER's defection was a great blow to the Tory party, and a singular disappointment to all his friends. For no one had entertained the least jealousy or suspicion of this part of his conduct. He had such an honest and open countenance as would have deceived the most skilful physiognomist. He was not a lover of money, nor did he seem ambitious of any thing, but true glory; and that he enjoyed. For no man within my memory was more esteemed and reverenced. He declared his principles very freely, and all his actions were correspondent. The Tories considered him as their chief: they placed the greatest confidence in him, and did nothing without his advice and approbation. They even persuaded themselves that he had an excellent judgment and understanding, though his parts were very moderate, and his learning superficial. But he was affable and courteous; and he had a certain plausibility, which, with a candour of manners, supplied the place of superior talents. He had a large estate, and was celebrated by all his neighbours for his hospitality. And he was as much respected for his private as he was for his public virtues. He was a good husband, a good father, and a good master. When he accepted the privy seal, he used all his art to preserve the good opinion of his old friends. He assured them, that he went into em-

ployment with no other view than to
serve his country, and that many articles
tending to a thorough reformation were
already stipulated. I had a letter from
him (for I lived in some degree of intimacy with him for many years) to the
purposes I have mentioned. Soon after
I saw him, when he read the articles to
me. If I rightly remember, they were
thirteen in number: not one of which
was performed, or ever intended to be
performed. When this was at length
discovered, he laid aside his disguise,
adhering to the new system, and openly
renouncing his old principles. He was
then created an Earl: and this feather
was the only reward of his apostacy.
For all the money which he received
from his place did not refund him half,

the sum (as he himself confessed) which
he had expended to support the measures of the administration. Such was
the conduct of this unhappy man, who
for a shadow bartered a most respectable
character, and sacrificed his honour and
his country. After this he never enjoyed
any peace of mind, and it is no wonder
if he died of what we call a broken
heart.

I WAS INVITED to dine at the late
Earl of MARCHMONT'S, where I found
the present Earl and his brother, my
Lord STAIRS, Sir LUKE SCHAUB, and
four or five ladies. The conversation
during dinner (occasioned by something
which had just then happened at court)
turned upon the Q——'s love of money.

Every one, except Sir Luke Schaub, had a story on this subject: and some of them were very unbecoming *sacred majesty*. Sir Luke, who was a pensioned courtier, thought himself obliged to defend the Q——'s honour, and said to me, who sat next him: " Doctor, there is not more than one of these scandalous tales in a hundred that is true." "Then, Sir Luke," I replied, "you acknowledge that one in a hundred is true." He immediately perceived his error: and one of the company observed, " that if only one in a hundred of such stories as had been related were true, there would not be any great injustice in imputing all the rest." It might perhaps be too severe a censure to charge a woman with unchastity, who had only

E

transgressed with one man; but a base and sordid spirit is discovered by one act of avarice.

THE CUSTOM of giving money to servants is now become such a grievance, that it seems to demand the interposition of the legislature to abolish it. How much are foreigners astonished, when they observe that a man cannot dine at any house in *England*, not even with his father or his brother, or with any other of his nearest relations, or most intimate friends and companions, unless he pay for his dinner! But how can they behold without indignation or contempt a man of quality standing by his guests, while they are distributing money to a double row of his servants? If, when I am in-

vited to dine with any of my acquaintance, I were to send the master of the
house a sirloin of beef for a present, it
would be considered as a gross affront;
and yet as soon as I shall have dined,
or before I leave the house, I must be
obliged to pay for the sirloin, which was
brought to his table, or placed on the
sideboard. For I contend that all the
money which is bestowed on the servants is given to the master. For if the
servants wages were increased in some
proportion to their vails (which is the
practice of a few great families, the D.
of NORFOLK'S, Mr. SPENCER'S, Sir FRAN-
CIS DASHWOOD'S, &c.), this scandalous
custom might be totally extinguished.
I remember a Lord POOR, a Roman
Catholic Peer of *Ireland*, who lived upon

a. small pension which Q. ANNE had granted him: he was a man of honour, and well esteemed; and had formerly been an officer of some distinction in the service of *France*. The Duke of OR-MONDE had often invited him to dinner, and he as often excused himself. At last the Duke kindly expostulated with him, and would know the reason why he so constantly refused to be one of his guests. My Lord POOR then honestly confessed that he could not afford it: " but," says he, " if your Grace will put a guinea into my hands as often as you are pleased to invite me to dine, I. will not decline the honour of waiting on you." This was. done; and my Lord was afterwards a frequent guest in St. James's Square. For my part, whenever

I am invited to the table of any of my noble friends, I have the vanity to imagine that my company is desired for the sake of my conversation; and there is certainly no reason why I should give the servants money because I give the master pleasure. Besides, I have observed the servants of every great house consider these vails to be as much their due as the fees which are claimed in the Custom-house, or in any other public office. And therefore they make no distinction between a gentleman of 200*l.* a year, and one of 2000*l.*; although they look on the former as inferior in every respect to themselves. *Maxima quæque domus - servis est plena superbis* is an axiom which will hold true to the end of the world. Upon the whole, if this custom, which is certainly a disgrace to our country, is to continue in force, I think it may at least be practised in a better manner. Suppose there were written in large gold letters over the door of every man of rank: THE FEES FOR DINING HERE ARE THREE HALF CROWNS [OR TEN SHILLINGS] TO BE PAID TO THE PORTER ON ENTERING THE HOUSE: PEERS OR PEERESSES TO PAY WHAT MORE THEY THINK PROPER. By this regulation two inconveniences would be avoided: first, the difficulty of distinguishing, amongst a great number, the quality of the servants. I, who am near-sighted, have sometimes given the footman what I designed for the butler, and the butler has had only the footman's fee: for which the butler treated me with no small contempt, until an opportunity offered of correcting my error. But, secondly, this method would prevent the shame which every master of a family cannot help feeling whilst he sees his guests giving about their shillings and half-crowns to his servants. He may then conduct them boldly to his door, and take his leave with a good grace. My Lord TAAFFE of *Ireland*, a general officer in the *Austrian* service, came into *England* a few years ago on account of his private affairs. When his friends, who had dined with him, were going away, he always attended them to the door; and if they offered any money to the servant who opened it (for he never suffered but one servant to appear), he always prevented them, saying, in his manner of speaking

English, " IF YOU DO GIVE, GIVE IT TO
ME, FOR IT WAS I THAT DID BUY THE
DINNER."

A PERFECT FRIENDSHIP, as it is de-
scribed by the ancients, can only be
contracted between men of the greatest
virtue, generosity, truth, and honour.
Such a friendship requires that all things
should be in common; and that one friend
should not only venture, but be ready to
lay down his life for the other. According to this definition of friendship, *Cicero*
observes that all the histories, from the
earliest ages down to his time, had not
recorded more than two or three pair of
friends; and I doubt whether at this
day we could add two or three pair more
to the number. In our country, which

is governed by money, and where every man is in pursuit of his own interest, it would be in vain to look for a real friendship. Our companions, and our common acquaintance, those especially with whom we live in any degree of familiarity, we call our friends; and we are always ready to give them such marks of our friendship as will not put us to any great inconveniency, or subject us to any great expense. If an Englishman, like the Greek philosopher, were to bequeath his wife and children to be maintained by one of his rich friends, he would be deemed *non compos.* If a man would long preserve his friendships, I mean those imperfect friendships which are generally contracted in this country, he should be particularly careful to have no money-concerns with his friends, at least to owe them no great obligations on that account. Most of the breaches of friend-ship which I have remarked, as likewise the family feuds which are now subsist-ing in *England*, are to be ascribed to this cause. The latter indeed are not always to be avoided, but the first always may. I was talking on this subject with a learned foreigner, who seemed to doubt the truth of my general observation, and thought my countrymen did not deserve the character which I had imputed to them. He could not conceive why there was not the greatest warmth and activity in our friendships, when we were so ready to relieve the helpless and indigent, and had given such proofs of our humanity and charity as were not equalled by any nation in *Europe*. And then he reckoned all the hospitals which were supported by annual and voluntary contributions. I acknowledged this to be a kind of a contradiction in our manners, but I did not tell him that I imputed no small proportion of these extraordinary charities to the vanity of the donors.

SUETONIUS, or whoever was the author of the Life of *Horace*, tells us that *Mecænas,* when he was dying, recommended *Horace* to the care of *Augustus Cæsar* in these words, *Horatii Flacci, ut mei, memor esto:* which in my judgment is the noblest and most beautiful expression of friendship that is recorded by any ancient or modern historian or biographer. I am so much affected by it, that in this short sentence I imagine I can discern the excellent qualities of the patron, and the great merit of the poet, as well as the force of their friendship.

DOCTOR SWIFT was always persuaded that the Archbishop of *York* had made impressions on Queen ANNE to his disadvantage, and by that means had obstructed his preferment in *England;* and he has hinted this in his Apology for the *Tale of the Tub,* and in other parts of his works; and yet my Lord BOLINBROKE, who must have been well informed of this particular, told me that he had been assured by the Queen herself, that she never had received any unfavourable character of Dr. SWIFT, nor had the Archbishop, or any other person, endeavoured to lessen him in her esteem. My Lord BOLINBROKE added, that this tale was invented by the Earl of *Ox-*

ford to deceive SWIFT, and make him contented with his Deanery in *Ireland;* which, although his native country, he always looked on as a place of banishment. If Lord BOLINBROKE had hated the Earl of *Oxford* less, I should have been readily inclined to believe him.

KING CHARLES II. after taking two or three turns one morning in St. *James's Park* (as was his usual custom), attended only by the Duke of *Leeds* and my Lord CROMARTY, walked up *Constitution Hill,* and from thence into *Hyde Park.* But just as he was crossing the road, the Duke of *York's* coach was nearly arrived there. The DUKE had been hunting that morning on *Hounslow Heath,* and was returning in his coach, escorted by a party of the guards, who, as soon as they saw the

King, suddenly halted, and consequently stopt the coach. The DUKE being acquainted with the occasion of, the halt, immediately got out of his coach, and, after saluting the King, said he was greatly surprised to find his Majesty in that place with such a small attendance, and that he thought his Majesty exposed himself to some danger. " No kind of danger, JAMES; for I am sure no man in *England* will take away my life to make you King."—This was the King's answer. The old Lord CROMARTY often mentioned this anecdote to his friends.

IN THE CIVIL WAR, my grandfather, Sir WILLIAM SMYTH, was governor of * Hillesdon House, near Buckingham,

* The siege of Hillesdon House is nowhere mentioned by my Lord CLARENDON. The noble historian and Sir W. Smyth were not good friends.

where the king had a small garrison. This place was besieged and taken by CROMWELL. But the officers capitulated to march out with their arms, baggage, &c. As soon as they were without the gate, one of Cromwell's soldiers snatched off Sir William Smyth's hat. He immediately complained to Cromwell of the fellow's insolence, and breach of the capitulation. "Sir," says Cromwell, "if you can point out the man, or I can discover him, I promise you he shall not go unpunished. In the mean time (taking off a new beaver, which he had on his head) be pleased to accept of this hat instead of your own."

I mention this incident for no other reason but as it may serve in some measure to illustrate Cromwell's character.

Nothing is more mistaken than the act of revenge when it concludes in murder. To murder your enemy is to make yourself miserable, and to make him happy. By his death, perhaps, you may hurt some of his friends or relations; but this was not your intention.

To revenge the community is another case, and the assassination of a tyrant is public justice. And yet if I had been Brutus, I could not have prevailed on myself to have been one of Cæsar's murderers.

Cardinal Richelieu, who said that *unfortunate* and *imprudent* are two words which signify the same thing, seems to have founded this maxim on the singular happiness of his own administration. He

was certainly a very great politician;,but
he had all the power as well as the whole
revenue of *France* at his disposal. He
had a regiment of guards for his own
person; and the favours which he was
constantly conferring on his officers and
domestics attached them to him, and
secured their fidelity. It must further
be considered, that he made no scruple
of removing any man out of the way
who would not implicitly submit to his
will, or who seemed in any respect to
disapprove his measures. *Voulez vous
être à moi?* was the question he asked
Mareschal BASSOMPIERRE, which because
the Mareschal did not readily and di-
rectly answer, he was sent the next
morning to the Bastile, where he was a
prisoner until the Cardinal's death, about

eighteen years. However, with all this power and caution the Cardinal was two or three times in great danger of his life, and owed his escape to his good fortune and presence of mind, and not to his foresight, or to any intelligence he had received of his enemy's designs. Let us consult history, or make our own observations for the space of a few years, and we shall be convinced that there is a fatality which attends the lives of some men (perhaps of us all), insomuch that with the greatest prudence and circumspection, and with the noblest endowments of the mind, they are not able to avert their misfortunes; and if they happen to be engaged in the service of the commonwealth, the performance of their duty shall subject them to an accusation, and their virtues and love of their country be construed into high crimes and misdemeanors. On the other hand, we may behold the dullest fellows, men without any talents or any one good quality, succeed in all their undertakings, and arrive so suddenly to wealth and honours, that they may be justly styled, as they generally are, the favourites of Fortune. If they enjoy any high office or public employment, even their negligence, their blunders, their corruption, shall turn to their advantage. I never remember any administration in this country that would not furnish us with many examples both of one and the other.

SOME LADIES of my acquaintance, who have a fine understanding and a turn to poetry, of which they are good judges, have often complained that they could not discover any great beauties in the Odes of HORACE, which are so much admired; although they have read the most celebrated translations (for they are unacquainted with the original) in *English*, *French*, and *Italian*. But the truth is, the Odes of HORACE never were nor ever can be translated, so as to display the beauties of the original, which wholly consist in the language and expression. In the thought or sentiment there is nothing extraordinary or more excellent than what may be found in the poems of his cotemporaries; but the language is inimitable, and I doubt whether the most learned critic of the Augustan age, allowing him the best taste as well as judg-

ment, could have mended a, single expression in any of the Odes, or even have
changed one word for a better. This is
what PETRONIUS calls the *curiosa feli-
citas* of HORACE; which two words are
as happily joined together as *simplex
munditiis:* and these four words are, perhaps, sufficient to characterise the poet,
and express the beauty of his style in his
own manner. I could never read the
first stanza in the *Carmen Seculare* without falling into a fit of devotion : and yet
when I read it in the best translation, it
does not affect me. Thus likewise those
beautiful odes *Donec gratus eram,* &c.
and *Quem tu, Melpomene,* &c. (of which
SCALIGER said he would rather be the
author than King of *Arragon*) rendered
into any modern language, do not seem

to deserve an hundredth part of the praise bestowed on the originals.

THE SINGULAR ESTEEM which some learned critics have always expressed for the works of HORACE became at last so fashionable, that scarce a man who affected the character of a polite scholar ever travelled ten miles from home without an HORACE in his pocket. The late E. of S. was such an admirer of HORACE that his whole conversation consisted of quotations out of that poet: in which he often discovered his want of skill in the Latin tongue, and always his want of taste. But the man whom I looked on (if I may be allowed the expression) as HORACE-mad, was one Dr. DOUGLAS, a physician of some note in *London*: I made an acquaintance with this gentleman on purpose that I might have a sight of his curious library (if it might be called a library) which was a large room full of all the editions of HORACE which had ever been published, as well as the several translations of that author into the modern languages. If there were any other books in this room, as there were a small number, they were only there for the sake of HORACE, and were on no other account valuable to the possessor but because they contained some parts of HORACE which had been published with select pieces or *excerpta* out of other Latin authors for the use of schools; or because the translations of some of the odes and satires were printed in miscellanies, and were not to be found any where else. However, I must acknowledge that the Doctor understood his author, whom he had studied with great care and application. Amongst other of his criticisms he favoured me with the perusal of a dissertation on the first ode, and a defence of * Dr. HARE's famous emendation of TE *doctarum*, &c. instead of ME.

A STORY TELLER is the most agreeable or the most disagreeable character we can meet with. A story, which is designed to entertain a polite company, should

---

* This emendation hath been given by the Dutch critics to Brockhusius. But I could never find it in any part of his works, and therefore the merit of it should justly be left to Dr. HARE.

See a note at the bottom of page 150 of a pamphlet, published 1723, entitled Scriptures vindicated from the misinterpretation of the Bishop of Bangor, &c.

always be .short, and, with a mixture of wit and humour, be told in good language. KING · CHARLES the Second, who had most excellent parts, had likewise a most agreeable manner of telling his stories; and SHEFFIELD, Duke of BUCKINGHAM, informs us, that the same story which he had· heard from the King five or six times he always heard with pleasure, as it was always embellished with some new circumstances. This was a happy talent, owing to a quick fancy and a lively imagination; for a frequent repetition of the same tale to the same persons, which at first was very entertaining, becomes at length insipid and ridiculous, and is apt to lessen the character of the man who tells it, even in the esteem of his friends, who ascribe that to the want of judgment or defect of understanding which should only be imputed to the loss of memory. I have been greatly abashed when I have caught myself endeavouring to entertain my friend with the same story which I had related to him a few days before: and I have sometimes resolved to cure myself of this infirmity of my old age, by restraining my conversation, and confining it to the news and business of the day, the manners of the times, &c.; and when I happen to be in the company of scholars, making observations on ancient and modern authors. But hitherto I have not prevailed on myself to pursue this prudent resolution; but am content to bear this reproach of my age in common with my equals. I remember only one old man who was quite free from any

imputation of this kind : he was a fellow
of the college in which I was educated,
and was an instructive and the most delightful companion I have ever known;
he had an inexhaustible fund of merry
tales, or rather he had such a fund of
wit, and such a quick and luxuriant imagination, that he was always capable of
producing something new and very entertaining; and as we rarely heard him
tell the same stories twice, we concluded
they were the fruits of a sudden inven-
tion. HORACE, I imagine, was a man
of this character; he was certainly a
pleasant and facetious companion, as we
may judge by the jollity of some of his
odes, and by the love which Augustus
and Mæcenas had conceived for him.
Among many other short stories he hath

left us two, which are not more diverting than they are instructive, the *Ibam fortè viâ sacrâ*, and the account of *Philippus* and the Crier, Epist. 7. B. 1. LUCIAN was a merry Greek; he is every where full of wit; his drollery is exquisite, and his satire is just: one of his short tales has been wrought by APULEIUS into a large volume. But of all the ancient authors of this character, I have a partiality for PETRONIUS. There is a certain grace and pleasantry peculiar to himself in whatever he relates: his history of the EPHESIAN MATRON is allowed by all the critics to be a master-piece: it is concise and elegant; it is simple and sublime: but what distinguishes the excellent judgment of the author, there is not a circumstance which can be added to it or

taken from it without lessening its value;
and MONSIEUR ST. EVREMOND, though
I acknowledge him to be an admirable
writer, and one of the greatest geniuses
which this or the last age hath produced,
hath yet, in my opinion, done no honour
to PETRONIUS by paraphrasing the EPHE-
SIAN MATRON, and lengthening the narrative. To learn a good manner of telling a story or relating any fact, jocose or
serious, we should be very conversant
with TERENCE; his comedies will furnish
many examples for our purpose: the first
scene in the *Andria* is a beautiful narrative, and in my judgment hath not been
equalled by any comic writer, ancient or
modern. CICERO hath remarked some
of its excellencies: and there are others
which cannot escape the observation of

any man of taste. The incident, which discovers the love of Pamphilus for *Glycerium*, is so descriptive, that whilst we are reading that part, we imagine ourselves present at the funeral pile : the whole scene is clear and methodical, and though it consists of two or three pages only, there are circumstances enough to supply some modern memoir-writers with matter for a whole volume.

A little before the revival of letters, BOCCACE and some other Italian wits began to publish short stories ; and from them our CHAUCER borrowed most o his Canterbury Tales. But whatever he took in hand of foreign growth he much improved, and adapted to the taste and manners of his own countrymen. Towards the end of the last century and the

beginning of this, FONTAINE and our
PRIOR published their tales, and it is
generally agreed that in this kind of
writing they have excelled all who went
before them.

But I have insensibly digressed from
my first purpose, which was only to mention some particular characters, which,
as I had observed, were capable of en-
livening or confounding a conversation
by their manner of telling a story; for a
man may be a facetious and witty author,
who is a dull and heavy companion. Such,
I am well assured, was the celebrated
FONTAINE, whom I have mentioned
above: and who that hath read Mr. AD-
DISON's Tatlers and Spectators, which
abound with wit and humour, and are
infinitely superior to all his other com-

positions, would not expect to have found him a most agreeable companion? An old acquaintance of mine hath treasured up a very curious and interesting collection of anecdotes, which have always given me great pleasure when I have been able to come at them; for though he is ever ready to tell his story, and likewise knows how to apply it, yet his introduction is so long and tedious, and his digressions so frequent, and so much out of the way, that he often loses his point of view, and is unable to recover the track, unless he asks the person who sits next him upon what occasion he began his tale; and yet this gentleman does not want either learning or prudence, and has kept as good company as any man in England. What is very remarkable, he is apt to condemn others for the fault of which he is so notoriously guilty; so little sensible are the wisest men of their own failings!

There are some persons who generally take the lead in conversation, and are well furnished for the purpose; but they relate nothing but what is wonderful, and they are always the heroes of their own romances: and like other heroes, they do not easily bear a contradiction; but are apt to quarrel if you doubt their honour, and seem incredulous. I knew a merry droll, who was always an overmatch for men of this character: whenever they advanced something very romantic, he always rose some degrees above them, and asserted a fact which was more astonishing and improbable than any thing which they had related. This is, perhaps, the best and safest method of answering a *gasconade*, and reproving the author. I will conclude with this observation : a story well told, and well applied, is not only the most delightful part of a private conversation, but is generally of good use in a public assembly where any important matter is to be debated ; for it embellishes the most eloquent oration ; it awakes and keeps up the attention of the audience ; it puts the adverse party into good humour, and has sometimes a greater weight and influence than the most powerful and persuasive arguments.

DEUS NOBIS HÆC OTIA FECIT hath been thought by some commentators a criminal compliment, and a piece of flattery

unworthy of VIRGIL. But they have
not sufficiently considered how this expression is explained and qualified by
the verse which immediately follows,
namque erit ille mihi semper Deus: for
here the poet seems to restrain the wor-
ship of AUGUSTUS to himself, and does
not require that he should be esteemed
a god by any other person. Besides,
this was not such a high flight in a *Roman* poet as it would be in an English
or French writer: many of the *Roman*
deities had been men, and all of them
were subject to human infirmities and
the passions of men, such as love, anger,
hatred, and revenge: so that it would
not have been a crime to have pronounced some of the most excellent citizens of *Rome* superior to many of their

gods; and Lucan has exalted Cato above them all, if I rightly comprehend the meaning of this verse,

Victrix causa Deis placuit, sed victa Catoni.

I am told that the * inscription placed over the gate of the Duke of Argyle's new house in *Scotland* is,

Dux Cumbriæ *nobis hæc otia fecit.*

This is a very improper motto or inscription for a house, and is on another account very absurd; for when we borrow a verse from a *Greek* or *Roman* poet, and adapt it to a modern purpose, by changing a word or two, we should be careful to fit the words we insert to the measure of the verse. Dux Cumbriæ will not stand

---

* I have been since informed that this is the inscription of the foundation stone.

in an hexameter. *Assuitur pannus.* It is prose and poetry ill pieced.

FLATTERY can never engage the attention of a judicious reader, unless it be short and very ingenious. The compliments which VIRGIL and HORACE have bestowed on their patrons are read with pleasure, and are the best examples of this kind of writing. The force and majesty of that beautiful *climax*, with which VIRGIL concludes his *Georgics*, cannot be sufficiently admired.

> *Cæsar dum magnus ad altum*
> *Fulminat Euphratem bello: Victorque volentes*
> *Per populos dat jura; viamque affectat Olympo.*

How comprehensive is this short compliment; and with what grace and dignity the poet rises, till he exalts his patron into a divinity! I may judge amiss, but I would rather have been the author of these three verses than PLINY's whole panegyric.

HORACE begins his Epistle to Augustus with great art and elegance of expression. The public character which he hath drawn of that prince in four or five short sentences, a modern dedicator would easily spin out into forty or fifty pages*.

I have often wondered how the custom of writing long dedications first prevailed; it must certainly be attributed to the ig-

* *Cum tot sustineas, et tanta negotia solus,*
Res Italas bello tuteris, moribus ornes,
Legibus emendes : in publica commoda peccem,
Si longo sermone morer tua tempora, CÆSAR.

N. B. The praises given to the Emperor in the end of this Epistle are as refined as those which I have cited.

norance rather than to the vanity of modern patrons.' To ascribe to a great man those virtues which he wants is in my opinion an injurious treatment: it is irony; it is satire; and hath sometimes been construed as such, and pronounced to be a libel by our courts of judicature. There is, moreover, this ill consequence resulting from it, that the patron's good qualities, if he happens to have any good qualities, are by this means obscured and discredited; for an heap of fulsome and false praise will always render that suspected which is true. When I take up a book which is dedicated to the King or a prince of the blood, or a prime minister, or indeed any man of great quality or great wealth, I always pass over the dedication, where I am sure of meeting

with nothing but the grossest flattery.
If I could say of our * KING what may
be said with great truth of the KING of
PRUSSIA,

Quem tu, Dea, tempore in omni
Omnibus ornatum voluisti excellere rebus,

would not this short eulogy be preferable
to all the public addresses, dedications,
poetical rhapsodies, and birth-day odes,
which have been composed in honour of
his Majesty since his accession to the
throne?

ALTHOUGH VIRGIL was a court poet,
and a favourite of AUGUSTUS, and was
not only rewarded, but enriched by that
Emperor's bounty, yet his principles were

* King George the Second.

republican. He retained a secret veneration for the patriot senators, and abhorred that venality and corruption by
which the first CÆSAR overturned the
liberties of his country, and fixed his
usurpation. There are two passages,
one in the 6th, and the other in the 8th
book of the *Æneid*, which sufficiently
prove my assertion. And I have some-
-times wondered why TUCCA and VARIUS
did not expunge them out of a compliment to the prince; but it is probable
that their principles of government (for
they were both men of a distinguished
character) were the same as the poet's,
whose work they were commissioned to
revise.

Vendidit hic auro patriam, dominumque potentem
Imposuit.

The commentators are generally of opinion that Virgil in this place alludes to Curio,. who sold *Rome* to Julius Cæsar,. and was the principal cause of the ruin of the Commonwealth. But whether he alludes to Curio or not, he certainly avows his own principles by placing in the most horrible region of his poetical hell the man who sells his country, and erects it into a tyranny. The other line in the 8th book,

Secretosque pios : his dantem jura Catonem,

is a noble encomium on Cato, than which nothing can be carried higher; for the poet does not only assign to Cato the first seat in the happy abodes, but he places him at the head of all the other blessed spirits as their guide and director.

The critics-and commentators seem to agree that VIRGIL does not mean CATO UTICENSIS, but Cato the Censor; and they all give the same reasons for their conjecture. First, they allege, that to have bestowed such particular praise on CATO UTICENSIS, who was the most obstinate and inveterate enemy of JULIUS CÆSAR, would have been a signal affront to AUGUSTUS; and, secondly, as CATO was guilty of suicide, he could not be admitted into the *Elysian* fields: but these reasons, I think, are not convincing; for was not the affront to AUGUSTUS as great by placing CURIO, the most useful of CÆSAR's friends, in hell, as honouring CATO with a seat in *Elysium?* and as to his suicide, which the *Romans* esteemed the noblest of all his actions, that could be no bar to his future happiness: the commentators forget that ÆNEAS met DIDO in the *Elysian* fields. But whether the poet designed this great dignity and pre-eminence in *Elysium* for CATO the CENSOR, or CATO UTICENSIS, or whether he purposely left it doubtful, it is certain that he designed it (choose which of the CATOS you please) for a republican and patriot spirit, for one who had been a constant and steady friend to virtue and his country.

MONSIEUR TOURNEFORT, and other judicious and candid travellers, who lived some time among the TURKS, and were diligent to inquire into the religion, customs, and manners of those people, speak of them very favourably. They acknowledge that the TURKS perform all the duties of their religion with a scrupulous

exactness, and particularly are so charitable, that they are always ready to
relieve any person who will make his
necessities known. MONSIEUR TOURNE-
FORT says, that he never saw a beggar
in *Turkey*. In truth, if we compare his
account of the *Turks* with the character
which he and some later travellers give
us of the *Greeks*, we have no reason to
be surprised that so few of the former
are proselyted to the faith of CHRIST;
and yet these men are better Christians
than are perhaps to be found in most
parts of Christendom. As I have observed before, they are not only eminent
for their charities, but upon all occasions
they are easy and ready to forgive one
another. They have no duels in that
country, nor is any man assassinated in

Turkey from a false principle of honour or revenge. They retain a grateful sense of any favours they have received. A TURK of some distinction, who had been a slave at *Leghorn,* and during his captivity in that city had been often relieved by an English merchant, and by whose means he was at last enabled to recover his liberty, met Mr. RANDOLPH (whose travels we have) some years after at *Negropont,* and knowing him to be an Englishman, treated him with the greatest kindness and generosity; and having procured him a passage on board a *Turkish* ship, he recommended him to the captain in these words: "*When you see this man, you see me; what you do to him, you do to me; and I will answer it, be it good or ill.*" What a simplicity and goodness of heart appears in this recommendation! For the rest, the TURKS are very temperate both in eating and drinking, and the luxury of a table is unknown even in the palace of their Emperor. They persecute no one on the account of his religion; and the inquisitions of Spain and Portugal they would abhor, as the temples of *Baal,* or the altars of *Busiris.* I may add, that on some occasions they offer up prayers to JESUS CHRIST, as to a great prophet. They, indeed, deny his divinity, which is in them much more excusable than the blasphemy of those *monkish orders,* who make their founders equal to our Saviour, and the miracles pretended to be wrought by them superior to the miracles of the gospel.

THE ANSWERS which were made by Mr. LEGGE and Mr. PITT to the addresses of the several corporations, who presented those gentlemen with gold boxes, are in a very different style and manner. Mr. LEGGE always answers with dignity and freedom; he professes, he promises to serve his country; he accepts of a place for that purpose, and you cannot help believing him to be in earnest. Mr. PITT answers with caution and reserve; his eyes are fixed on the KING; he goes into employment on purpose to serve him, and thinks it his greatest happiness to execute his Majesty's gracious intentions. If Mr. PITT flatters the King, he is a bad man; if he does not, he is a bad patriot.

I BEGAN THE TOAST in anger, but I finished it in good humour. When I had concluded the second book, I laid aside the work, and I did not take it up again till some years after, at the pressing. instances of DR. SWIFT. In the last letter which I received from him, he writes thus : " *In malice I hope your law-suit will force you to come over* [to Dublin] *the next term, which I think is a long one, and will allow you time to finish it ; in the mean time I wish I could hear of the progress and finishing of another affair* [the TOAST] *relating to the same law-suit, but tryed in the courts above, upon a hill with two heads, where the defendants will as infallibly and more effectually be cast,*" &c. And speaking of this work to a lady, his near relation, who is now living, after he had

H

perused the greatest part of it in the manuscript, he told her, *if he had read the* TOAST *when he was only twenty years of age, he never would have wrote a satire.* It is no wonder that such a singular approbation should raise the vanity of a young writer, or that I imagined I wanted no other vindication of this per-formance than DR. SWIFT's opinion. He was chiefly pleased with the notes, and expressed his surprise that I had attained such a facility in writing the burlesque Latin. The motives which induced me to form the notes in that manner, was the judgment I made of those on Mr. POPE's *Dunciad.* That poem, it must be allowed, is an excellent satire ; but there is little wit or humour in the notes, although there is a great affectation of both. After Dr. Swift's testimonial, I ought, perhaps, to esteem the Toast above all my other works; however, I must confess there are some parts of it which my riper judgment condemns, and which I wish were expunged: particularly the description of Mira's person in the third book is fulsome, and unsuitable to the polite manners of the present age. But if this work was more exceptionable than my enemies pretend it is, I may urge for my excuse, that although it has been printed more than thirty years, yet it has never been published: I have, indeed, presented a few copies to some friends, on giving me their honour that they would not suffer the books to go out of their hands without my consent. One of these persons,

however, forfeited his honour in the
basest manner, by putting his copy into
the hands of BLACOW, and the rest of
the Oxford informers; but as they had
no key to the work, and did not understand or know how to apply the characters, they were content to call it an execrable book, and throw dirt at the author:
and this, in their judgment, is the most
effectual way of answering any performance of wit and humour.

AVARICE, says the author of RELIGIO
MEDICI, *seems to me not so much a vice,
as a deplorable piece of madness;* and if
he had added *incurable,* his definition
would have been perfect; for an ava-
ricious man is never to be cured unless
by the same medicine which perchance

may cure a mad dog. The arguments of reason, philosophy, or religion, will little affect him ; he is born and framed to a sordid love of money, which first appears when he is very young, grows up with him, and increases in middle age, and when he is old, and all the rest of his passions have subsided, wholly engrosses him. The greatest endowments of the mind, the greatest abilities in a profession, and even the quiet possession of an immense treasure, will never prevail against avarice. My LORD HARDWICK, the late Lord Chancellor, who is said to be worth 800,000*l.* sets the same value on half a crown now as he did when he was only worth one hundred. That great captain, the DUKE of MARLBOROUGH, when he was in the last stage of life, and very infirm, would walk from the public rooms in *Bath* to his lodgings in a cold dark night to save sixpence in chair hire. If the Duke, who left at his death more than a million and a half sterling, could have foreseen that all his wealth and honours were to be inherited by a grandson of my Lord *Trevor*'s, who had been one of his enemies, would he have been so careful to save sixpence for the sake of his heir? Not for the sake of his heir; but he would always have saved a sixpence. Sir JAMES LOWTHER, after changing a piece of silver in George's Coffee-house, and paying twopence for his dish of coffee, was helped into his chariot (for he was then very lame and infirm), and went home; some little time after he returned to the same coffee-house on purpose to acquaint the woman who kept it that she had given him a bad halfpenny, and demanded another in exchange for it. Sir JAMES had about 40,000*l*. per annum, and was at a loss whom to appoint his heir. I knew one Sir THOMAS COLBY, who lived at Kensington, and was, I think, a commissioner in the victualling-office; he killed himself by rising in the middle of the night when he was in a very profuse sweat, the effect of a medicine which he had taken for that purpose, and walking down stairs to look for the key of his cellar, which he had inadvertently left on a table in his parlour: he was apprehensive that his servants might seize the key and rob him of a bottle of port wine. This man died intestate, and left more than 200,000*l*. in the funds, which was shared among five or six day-labourers, who were his nearest relations. Sir WILLIAM SMYTH of Bedfordshire, who was my kinsman, when he was near seventy, was wholly deprived of his sight: he was persuaded to be couched by TAYLOR, the oculist, who by agreement was to have sixty guineas if he restored his patients to any degree of sight: TAYLOR succeeded in his operation, and Sir WILLIAM was able to read and write without the use of spectacles during the rest of his life; but as soon as the operation was performed, and Sir WILLIAM perceived the good effects of it, instead of being overjoyed, as any other person would have been, he began to lament the loss (as he called it) of his sixty guineas. His contrivance therefore now

was how to cheat the oculist: he pretended that he had only a glimmering,
and could see nothing perfectly; for that
reason the bandage on his eye was continued a month longer than the usual
time: by this means he obliged TAYLOR
to compound the bargain, and accept of
twenty guineas; for a covetous man thinks
no method dishonest which he may legally
practise to save his money. Sir WILLIAM
was an old bachelor, and at the time
TAYLOR couched him had a fair estate
in land, a large sum of money in the
stocks, and not less than 5000 or 6000 in
his house. But to conclude this article;
all the dramatic writers, both ancient and
modern, as well as the keenest and most
elegant satirists, have exhausted their
whole stock of wit to expose avarice;

this is the chief subject of Horace's satires and epistles; and yet the character of a covetous man hath never yet been fully drawn or sufficiently explained. The EUCLIO of PLAUTUS, the L'AVARE of MOLIERE, and the MISER of SHADWELL, have been all exceeded by some persons who have existed within my own knowledge. If you could bestow on a man of this disposition the wealth of both the *Indies*, he would not have ENOUGH; because by ENOUGH (if such a word is to be found in the vocabulary of Avarice) he always means something more than he is possessed of. CRASSUS, who had a yearly revenue sufficient to maintain a great army, perished, together with his son, in endeavouring to add to his store. In the fable of MIDAS, the poet had exhibited a complete character, if MIDAS, instead of renouncing the gift which the god had bestowed on him, had chosen to die in the act of creating gold.

I HAVE LATELY READ a small volume in *octavo*, which hath been universally well received; so that in the space of a year there were published no less than six editions of this book; and yet there is nothing to be found in it that is new; but the author hath judiciously collected the thoughts and sentiments of our best political writers, which he hath displayed with so much art, and hath methodised and arranged in such an agreeable order, and in so neat a style, that he seems to have made every thing his own. The scope of this work is to prove, that all the misfortunes which happened to us the beginning of the present war are to be ascribed to our effeminacy and luxury, which are the necessary consequences of that system of corruption by which we now are governed. I should have conceived a very high opinion of this writer, and have esteemed the man as much as his work, if he had not been guilty of such base adulation; especially if he had not flattered one of the great patrons of that corruption which he hath so justly complained of and exposed. If I were to write a satire against gaming, and in the middle of my work insert a panegyric on the clubs at ARTHUR'S, who would not question the good intentions of the author? and who would not condemn the absurdity of such a motley piece? *Humano capiti*, &c.

A PRIME MINISTER, who has a little mind and a weak judgment, makes a hundred promises, which are neither in his abilities or in his intentions to perform : he is despised by his own instruments and levee-hunters, and hated by all the rest of the nation ; he is incapable of forming or executing any great or glorious design ; he has only one thing in view, which is to preserve his power by a corrupt majority in the House of Commons : for this reason he prefers his followers out of mere necessity, who never think themselves obliged to him for the places and pensions which they enjoy. The D. of N. hath spent half a million, and made the fortunes of five hundred men, and yet is not allowed to have one real friend.

E CŒLO DESCENDIT, ΓΝΩΘΙ ΣΕΑΥΤΟΝ, is an article of my creed; and certainly to know one's self is the perfection of human knowledge, and the man who hath early attained it will pass through life with ease and tranquillity. CICERO, in an epistle to his brother, hath well explained this precept, *præceptum illud noli putare ad arrogantiam minuendam solum esse dictum, verum etiam, ut bona nostra norimus.* To know ourselves is to be as truly sensible of our good as of our bad qualities; and whilst we endeavour to free ourselves from the last, to know how to apply the first in the conduct of life. I have been acquainted with men of wit and learning, and whose morals were irreproachable, who were little acquainted with themselves, who so egregiously mistook their own talents as to leave or

resign into the hands of others affairs
of importance which they could have
finished with honour and profit, in order
to go into a business of which they were
totally ignorant. If Mr. ADDISON had
entered into holy orders (and he had
made divinity his chief study), he might
have placed himself as high as he pleased
on the bench of bishops; in that station
he would have done honour to the hierarchy, and would have been a principal
ornament of the Church of England: but
he ambitioned to be a minister of state,
and because he had some talents, which
no man in the administration possessed,
he thought himself capable of filling the
first employments in the government.
This also seemed to be the opinion of
his friends and patrons, and upon this

presumption he was appointed Secretary of State: but he soon found himself incapable of performing the duty of his office; for though he understood the foreign languages, and could write his own with purity, elegance, and correctness, yet he could not speak a word in the house of parliament; and, which is more surprising, he could not dictate the common letters of business which were necessary to be sent from his office; he was, therefore, to his great mortification, obliged to resign it, and content himself with a sinecure, the place of a Teller in the Exchequer, during the rest of his life. I knew Mr. ARESKINE, my Lord MARR's brother; he was one of the judges in Scotland, and was much esteemed for his abilities and knowledge in the laws of his country. His station, in virtue of which he was called LORD GRANGE *, was honourable, was for life; and such a salary was annexed to it as would enable a man to live in ease and affluence in that part of the world. However he was by no means satisfied with this office; and therefore, to render himself more conspicuous, he determined to get a seat in the House of Commons; though to effect this, he was previously obliged to resign his judgeship. However, he made no doubt of soon acquiring by his oratory some great and lucrative em-

* The Duke of Argyle, as soon as he was informed that my LORD GRANGE had taken his measures so well as to be sure of being elected into parliament, brought a bill into the House of Lords, which easily passed both Houses, to disqualify any judge of Scotland to sit in the House of Commons.

ployment in England: his first speech was much applauded, for he understood business, and argued justly; but the House would not long endure his *Scotch* accent; so that after speaking three or four times he was ill heard and neglected. In the next parliament he lost his election; and I met him in London a year or two before he died, when he was so reduced in his circumstances that he was scarce able to furnish himself with the necessaries of life. Upon recollection I could instance some other persons of great abilities, who have either suffered a signal disgrace, or have ruined their fortunes, for want of inspecting more nearly into themselves; and I do not know whether I may not be justified if I insert the name of Lord George Sackville in '

my catalogue: but not in consequence of
the sentence pronounced against him by
the court martial (for it was a very extraordinary proceeding to judge a man
first and try him afterwards,) but from
the unprejudiced relation of some officers
of honour and integrity, who had been
with my Lord in action, and had remarked
his conduct. But notwithstanding the
characters I have here mentioned, I cannot easily believe it would be very difficult for a man to be so familiar with himself as to know what he can or can not
do, *quid ferre recusent—Quid valeant hu-
meri.* It is indeed the peculiar happiness
of this country, that all who have any
share in the administration of public
affairs are equally fit for all employment. His Grace of N. was first Cham-

berlain, then Secretary of State, and
is now First Commissioner of the Trea-
sury and Chancellor of Cambridge; and
all these high employments he hath executed with equal capacity and judgment,
without being indebted to age or experience for the least improvement; and
if he had been pleased to accept the
Archbishopric of Canterbury, when it
was lately vacant, he would have proved
himself as great an orator in the pulpit
as he is in the senate, and as able a divine
as he is a politician. As often as I hear
this nobleman named, he puts me in
mind of a certain Irish baronet, a man
of some interest in his country, who when
the Duke of ORMONDE was appointed
Lord Lieutenant of *Ireland* in the beginning of Queen ANNE's reign, desired

his Grace to give him a bishopric, or a regiment of horse, or to make him Lord Chief Justice of the King's Bench.

A TRIFLING INCIDENT hath sometimes been the occasion of the greatest quarrels, and such as have ended fatally. I remember two gentlemen, who were constant companions, disputing one evening at the Grecian Coffee-house concerning the accent of a Greek word. This dispute was carried to such a length that the two friends thought proper to determine it with their swords; for this purpose they stept out into Devereux Court, where one of them (whose name, if I rightly remember, was FITZGERALD) was run through the body, and died on the spot. Some gentlemen and ladies of two noble families in Scotland, who were near relations, and had always lived together in the greatest harmony and friendship, supt with me in St. Mary Hall. A very innocent joke, which was designed by the present Earl of M. who was one of the company, to increase our mirth and good humour, was highly resented by one of the ladies, and afterwards improved by her into such a quarrel, as concluded in an open rupture between the two families.

I. G. my old acquaintance, and one Mr. E. of Bristol, both single men, and in good health and good circumstances, agreed to travel together for three or four years, and visit all the countries of Europe; for that purpose they provided themselves with passports, bills of ex-

change, letters of credit and recommendation, &c. About six or seven days
after they set out, they arrived at Brussels, where they had for supper a woodcock and a partridge; they disputed long
which of the birds should be cut up first,
and with so much heat and animosity,
that if they had not both been gentlemen
of a *well-tempered* courage, this silly dispute might have terminated as unhappily
as the affair at the *Grecian* Coffee-house.
To such an height however the quarrel
arose, that they did not only renounce
their new design of travelling, but all
friendship and correspondence; and the
next morning they parted, and returned
to *England*, one by the way of Calais,
and the other through *Holland*. About
half a year afterwards I happened to be

in **I. G.'s** company; I asked him whether
what I had heard was true, that he and
E—TON had agreed to make the tour of
Europe together, but had unfortunately
quarrelled the first week about cutting
up a woodcock and a partridge. " *Very*
true," says he; " *and did you ever know*
such an absurd fellow as E—TON, who in-
sisted on cutting up a woodcock before a
partridge * *?*" If my old acquaintance
had not made me this answer, I should
not, I believe, have told this story. These
relations may serve to give a foreigner
some idea of those many odd and singular characters which are so justly imputed to the English nation.

* If we were carefully to trace the descent of
these whimsical heads, we should generally discover
a madness in the family.

ILLE CRUCEM TULIT, HIC DIADEMA, is
what must frequently happen in every
corrupt administration; and was lately
verified by the sentence of the court
martial which tried Admiral BING, and
the honours which at the same time were
conferred on the Governor of *Minorca*.
I speak this upon a supposition that
BING was justly put to death; of which
a doubt will always remain with us, and
which our posterity will scarce believe,
since, in the judgment of those very
gentlemen who condemned this unfortunate admiral, he deserved nothing
worthy of death or of bonds. Admiral
FORBES, one of the Lords of the Ad-
miralty, who refused to concur with the
rest of his brethren, hath given such reasons for his dissent, as sufficiently de-
monstrate the absurdity of their sentence,

to say no worse of it. But whether Mr. BING suffered justly or not, it is apparent to the whole nation that those ministers who took no care to supply the garrison of Port *Mahon,* after they had received certain advice of the intended invasion, were the greater criminals. May it not be fairly inferred that BING was sacrificed to appease the clamour of the people, and to screen his superiors?

WHOEVER HATH READ the History of the five James's, and attentively considered the great misfortunes which have befallen the HOUSE of STUART *, both before and since the crown of England

* Si quelque chose justifie ceux, qui croient une fatalité, à laquelle rien ne se peut se soustraire, c'est cette suite continuelle de malheurs qui persécuta la Maison de Stuart pendant plus de trois cent années.
VOLTAIRE, *Louis XIV.*

was settled on the princes of that name, must acknowledge that an evil fate hath constantly pursued them, and seems determined never to leave their family till every branch of it be extinguished. If I were to ascribe their calamities to another cause, or endeavour to account for them by any natural means, I should think they were chiefly owing to a certain obstinacy of temper, which appears to have been hereditary, and inherent in all the STUARTS, except CHARLES II. I have read a series of letters which passed between King CHARLES I., whilst he was prisoner at *Newcastle*, and his queen, who was then in *France*. The whole purport of her letters was to press him most earnestly to make his escape, which she had so well contrived, by the assistance of Cardinal Mazarin, that it could not fail of success. She informed him of the designs of his enemies, and assured him, if he suffered himself to be conveyed to London, they would certainly put him to death. But all her entreaties were fruitless: she could not persuade him to believe her informations. In all his answers he was positive that his enemies would not dare to attempt his life. This king was certainly a most religious and virtuous man; but he had conceived too high a notion of his prerogative, and he wanted all the arts of government. The same thing may truly be said of King JAMES II. whose misfortunes have generally been ascribed, both by his friends and enemies, not so much to his bigotry*, as to the ill judgment which he made of men and things, and which was not to be convinced or controlled by any remonstrances. I was talking with the old Lord Granard, whom I knew formerly in Ireland, concerning the revolution. He told me, that the first night he arrived at the camp on Salisbury Plain, where King James was then with his army, and where my Lord Granard had the command of a regiment, that CHURCHILL (the late Duke of Marlborough) and some other colonels invited him to supper, and opened to him their design of deserting to the PRINCE of ORANGE. My Lord GRANARD did not

* But his ill judgment was perhaps the effect of his bigotry. See the next note.

only refuse to enter into the confederacy, but went immediately to the KING, and told him he was betrayed, acquainting him with the discourse which had passed at supper. At the same time he advised the KING to seize all the conspirators, and give their commands to other officers, of whose fidelity he could be well assured. If this advice had been followed, King WILLIAM's attempt had probably been defeated; but the KING did not seem to give any credit to my Lord Granard's story, and neglected to make a present inquiry into an affair of such great importance. The next morning he was convinced of his error, when it was too late to apply a remedy. I could mention other anecdotes, which I heard from some Roman Catholic gentlemen in Ireland, relating to King James's* conduct, which would make it evidently appear that he lost that kingdom by the same obstinacy and wrong judgment by which he was deprived of the crown of England. And

* King JAMES II. was a good Englishman, and a lover of his country, and was perhaps less ambitious and less desirous of absolute power than his successor. If he had been indifferent in matters of religion, or had professed the same faith with the Emperor of *China,* he would have proved one of the best princes who have governed the British islands. But his great bigotry obscured all his good qualities; and his zeal to introduce popery was so violent, and prompted him to such extravagant attempts, as must necessarily, if they had succeeded, have ended in the total ruin, not only of our religious, but our civil liberties. This king's intemperate zeal was ridiculed even by the court of Rome. And how must he have been mortified, if, upon his first appearance at Versailles, after his abdication, he had heard Cardinal —— say to the person who stood next him, " see the man who lost three kingdoms for an old mass!"

now I could derive the same character down to his grandson, who made such a figure in 1745, if, for the better informa- tion of my countrymen, I were at liberty to relate some recent transactions, *quæque ipse miserrima vidi—et quorum pars magna fui.*

A REPARTEE, or a quick and witty answer to an insolent taunt, or to any ill-natured or ironical joke or question, is always well received (whether in a public assembly or a private company) by the persons who hear it, and gives a reputation to the man who makes it. CICERO, in one of his letters to ATTICUS, informs him of some reproaches, a kind of coarse raillery, which passed between himself and CLODIUS in the senate, and seems to exult and value himself much on his own repartees: though I do not think that this was one of Cicero's excellencies. ATTERBURY, Bishop of *Rochester*, when a certain hill was brought into the House of Lords, said among other things, *" that he prophesied last winter this bill would be attempted in the present session, and he was sorry to find that he had proved a true prophet."* My Lord CONINGSBY, who spoke after the bishop, and always spoke in a passion, desired the house to remark, *" that one of the Right Reverend had set himself forth as a prophet; but for his part he did not know what prophet to liken to, unless to that furious prophet* BALAAM, *who was reproved by his own ass."* The bishop in a reply, with great wit and calmness, exposed this rude attack, concluding

thus: *" since the noble. Lord hath discovered in our manners such a similitude,
I am well content to be compared to the
prophet BALAAM: but, my Lords, I am at
a loss how to make out the other part of the
parallel: I am sure that I have been reproved by nobody but his Lordship."*

When the late Earl of CADOGAN was
sent on an embassy to *Vienna,* he was
one day invited by Prince EUGENE to
be present at a review of the AUSTRIAN
Cuirassiers, which were a body of ten
thousand horse, and said to be the finest
troops in Europe: during the review,
Prince EUGENE turned to an *English*
officer, who had accompanied my Lord
CADOGAN, and asked him if he thought
*" that any ten thousand English horse
could beat those Austrians."*—" *I do not
know, Sir,"* says the *English* officer,

" *whether they could or not : but I know that five thousand would try.*" This was a spirited answer, and such as the question deserved; for in this instance the prince seemed to have dropt his politeness.

I WAS AT TUNBRIDGE in 1758, where I met with the Chevalier Taylor, the famous oculist. He seems to understand the anatomy of the eye perfectly well; he has a fine hand and good instruments, and performs all his operations with great dexterity; for the rest, *Ellum homo confidens!* who undertakes any thing (even impossible cases) and promises every thing. No charlatan ever appeared with fitter and more excellent talents, or to a greater advantage; he has a good person,

is a natural orator, and has a facility of
learning foreign languages. He has travelled over all *Europe*, and always with
an equipage suitable to a man of the
first quality, and hath been introduced
to most of the sovereign princes, from
whom he has received many marks of
their liberality and esteem, titles, orders,
medals, rings, pictures, &c. He is an
honorary member of many foreign universities, and has published his works
in Latin, English, French, Spanish, and
Italian. He pretends to know the se-
crets of all courts, and to be as skilful
a politician as he is an oculist. He returned to *England*, as he told me, in
hopes of being immediately introduced
to his * Majesty, and recommended as

* King George II.

the only person able to cure the King's
eyes; but he has not hitherto succeeded
in this attempt, nor in other respects
been so highly considered by his own
countrymen as by foreign nations. The
following character, which I had drawn
of him, he entreated me to publish, as
what he conceived would do him honour.

ELOGIUM.

HIC EST, HIC VIR EST,

Quem docti, indoctique omnes impensè mirantur,

JOHANNES TAYLOR;

Cæcigenorum, cæcorum &, cæcutientium

Quotquot sunt ubique,

Spes unica, solamen, salus...

Quorum causâ,

Cunctas Europæ peragravit regiones;

Neque usquam gentium fuit hospes,

Nisi in patriâ suâ.

Russicis, Suecicis, Lusitanicis,

Titulis, phaleris, torquibus

Decorus incedit:

Totoque orbe nemini cuiquam ignotus, . . .
Nisi sibi.

Orator summus non factus, sed natus,
Vocis, perinde atque manûs, celeritate insignis,
Scit Latinè, Gallicè, Italicè, Germanicè fari,
Omnes callens linguas
Æquè-ac sermonem patrium.

Vultu compto, corpore procero, fronte urbanâ glo-
riosus,
Ingenioque præditus prope singulari,
Artem amandi, et amoris remedium
Plenius et melius Nasone ipso
Edidicit, docuit, exercuit.

Mirificus fabulator, magnificus promissor,
Rerum copiâ, artiumque varietate abundans,
Sese exhibet, effert, prædicat
In gymnasiis, in gynæceis, in conviviis, in triviis;
Philosophando gloriam magnam adeptus,
Maximam saltando.

In peregrinis civitatibus
Equos, servosque innumeros, quos vix Satrapes
Potest habere,
Ille alit.
Domi verò,

Quæ est moderatio animi sui,
Uno vili mancipio
Contentus vivit.

In celeberrimas coöptatus est Academias:
Neque tamen moribus, neque vultu, neque vestitu,
Videtur Academicus.

Regnorum omnium arcana scrutari potuit:
Neque tamen speculator sagax;
Neque regis cujusquam legatus,
Neque usquam fuit vir aulicus.

Præmia, dona, permulta, amplissima accepit;
Permulta corrasit, pecuniæ appetentior:
Et nondum, eheu! locupletatur.

Plures scripsit libros, quàm quivis possit legere:
Qui facinoribus tamen suis egregiis
Haud sufficiunt enumerandis.

Sexcentis primariis viris lumina reddidit:
Plusquam sexcentis, sed plebeiis,
Sed miseris, ademit.

Tum verò civibus suis præcipuè colendus,
Tum carminibus, docte * MORELLE, tuis celebrandus,

* Qui laudes hujus ophthalmici cecinit carminibus Græcis et Anglicanis.

Tum diplomatibus honorificis, & muneribus regiis
          donandus; . I
Si Cæsarem nostrum, pium, fortem, semper Augus-
          tum,
          Faceret benè oculatum,
     Et malos, siqui sunt, consiliarios
          Tiresiâ cæciores *.

THERE IS NO PLACE I have ever seen
which I review with so much pleasure
and satisfaction as the place of my school
education†, and the scenes of my boyhood.

* I have had an opportunity since this ELOGIUM
was written of viewing our Chevalier more nearly,
and considering him with greater attention. I have
therefore been able to improve the ELOGIUM, and
add some new features to his portrait; of which I
have printed a few copies to oblige my friends.

† My mother having died of the small-pox when
I was about seven years old, I was sent by my grandfather, Sir WILLIAM SMYTH, to Salisbury, and
placed under the care of Mr. TAYLOR, the master of
the free-school, in that city. There were at that
time two very flourishing schools in Salisbury.

I feel a thrilling secret joy in every street I pass through. How many agreeable trifles and little amusements do I recollect at almost every step! All my actions were then very innocent, and my errors and follies excusable: not so after I had entered into the great world!

Mr. LESLEY, a very eminent nonjuring clergyman, the author of the Rehearsals, and of many other political and controversial tracts during the reigns of King WILLIAM and Queen ANNE, left two sons, with whom I was intimately acquainted. They were both men of good parts and learning; but in their disposition and manners they were so very different, that they did not seem to be of the same family, nor even of the same nation.. The elder brother was overbearing and talkative; and, though he was sometimes an agreeable companion, yet he oftener tired and disgusted his company. He was so careless of his private affairs, that he could never be prevailed on to examine his agent's accounts. I have sometimes jocularly asked him if he knew the value of our coin, or the real difference between a piece of copper and a piece of silver of the same weight; for often, when I have been walking with him in the streets, he has given a beggar, who importuned him for an halfpenny, half a crown (for he always gave the first piece that came to his hand); but not from any principle of charity, but merely from his contempt of money, and to be rid of the beggar's importunity ; so that a small number of artful mendicants would often watch his motions, and, by this means empty his pockets before he returned home.

* -ROBIN to beggars, with a curse,
Flings the last shilling in his purse :
And, when the coachman comes for pay,
The rogue must call another day.

Young HARRY, when the poor are pressing,
Gives them a penny, and God's blessing ;
But, always careful of the main,
With twopence left walks home in rain.

HARRY LESLEY, the younger brother, who had been a colonel in the Spanish army, was grave, modest, and very well bred. He seldom talked of any thing

* This is part of a manuscript poem, written by Dr. SWIFT, in which, in his humorous manner, he has drawn a character of the two brothers.

which he did not perfectly understand; and he was always heard with pleasure. With an estate, worth about 500*l.* per annum, he made a good figure, kept a very hospitable table, and was universally esteemed by all his neighbours and acquaintance; for he was a gentleman of great honour and probity, and great goodness of heart. In his last sickness he ordered his manuscripts to be sent to me: amongst which are many essays which are worthy of being offered to the public.

BAXTER'S PHÆNOMENON of DREAM-ING hath given me greater satisfaction than any thing else which I have read on the same subject: and yet there are many objections which may be made to his hypothesis. And it seems to me a certain truth, that both our reason and philosophy must ever be puzzled how to account for the operations of our souls when we are sleeping; very often, indeed, when we are awake: for without a bribe, and when we are not urged by any governing passion, we find ourselves, on many occasions, impelled, by an irresistible fatality, to act contrary to the dictates both of our reason and our conscience. *Novi meliora proboque—Deteriora sequor* may, I fear, be said with truth of the whole human species: at least, upon a strict examination of ourselves, our friends, and acquaintance, we shall discover but few characters which are exempt from this imputation. But to return to the phænomenon of dreams:

we must either contradict all history,
both sacred and profane, or we must
agree that our souls, at some times, seem
to exercise, in our dreams, a very extraordinary intuitive faculty; and either
by their own powers are able to discover
future events, or, according to BAXTER's
system, by the information of other spirits. I do not discredit the story of
BRUTUS and his evil genius; but I believe the whole to have passed in a dream,
although BRUTUS might think himself
awake. CICERO's recal from banishment
was foretold in a dream, which he has
recited; but for which he endeavours
to account in an unphilosophical, and,
indeed, in a very absurd manner. And
because he was of a sect whose first principles were to doubt of every thing, he

would not, therefore, acknowledge a truth which he had experienced in himself. I have as little superstition as any man living, and I acknowledge that there is generally great confusion and incoherence in our dreams, and that many ridiculous scenes are in those hours obtruded on us. But, however, I cannot help concluding, from my own experience, that some of our dreams are the effect of a divine agency. The most interesting and most important occurrence of my whole life was foretold me in a dream; though it was not verified till thirty years after the prediction.

I DO NOT KNOW any better rules or maxims than the three following, which were framed by the old monk, to enable

a man to pass through life with ease and
security :

Nunquam malè loqui de superioribus.
Fungi officio taliter qualiter.
Sinere insanum mundum vadere, quò vult ; nam vult
vadere, quò vult.

The first of these may be greatly improved by adding St. ——'s precept, *To
speak evil of no man.*   And whoever is so
happy, either from his natural disposition
or his good judgment, constantly to observe this precept, will certainly acquire
the love and esteem of the whole community of which he is a member.   But
such a man is the *rara avis in terris;*
and, among all my acquaintance, I have
known only one person to whom I can
with truth assign this character.   The
person I mean is the present Lord Pit-

SLIGO of *Scotland*. I not only never heard this gentleman speak an ill word of any man living, but I always observed him ready to defend any other person who was ill spoken of in his company. If the person accused were of his acquaintance, my Lord PITSLIGO would always find something good to say of him as a counterpoise. If he were a stranger, and quite unknown to him, my lord would urge in his defence the general corruption of manners, and the frailties and infirmities of human nature.

It is no wonder that such an excellent man, who, besides, is a polite scholar, and has many other great and good qualities, should be universally admired and beloved, insomuch, that I persuade myself he has not one enemy in the world.

At least, to this general esteem and affection for his person his preservation must be owing. For, since his attainder*, he has never removed far from his own house, protected by men of different principles, and unsought for and unmolested by the government.

IT WAS AN absurd attempt of those controversial writers, who endeavoured to prove, against *Warburton*, that the ancient JEWS believed the doctrine of a future state; since there is not any

---

* It was not ambition, but a love for his country, and a conscientious regard to his duty, which drew this honest man (however he might be mistaken) into the rebellion of 1745. A great prince, who had been well informed of my Lord PITSLIGO's character, would immediately have pardoned him, and have restored the little estate which he had forfeited.

where in the books of *Moses* so much
as a distant hint of this doctrine. The
whole of the *Jewish* religion is comprised
in the ten commandments; and, if we
believe that these laws were delivered to
Moses by God himself, we must likewise
believe that God himself determined that
the JEWS should remain altogether ignorant of a future state. In these laws
the punishment which is threatened, and
the rewards which are promised, are
limited to this life only; for, although
offenders are threatened to be punished
in their posterity, even to the third and
fourth generation, yet this denunciation
of God's vengeance would probably little
influence or restrain the actions of a
wicked man, who knew he should himself be insensible of the punishment

which was to be inflicted. *Warburton,* indeed, to support his favourite hypothesis, declares his opinion, that this punishment, denounced against the posterity of those Jews who transgressed, was more terrible to them than any personal punishment. But this is a *postulatum* which cannot be granted, and may easily be disproved.

The promise of long. life to a people who had no prospect after it, and who believed they were to die as the beasts of the field, might be an inducement to virtue, and to an obedience of the laws. But was this promise always fulfilled? Were not the best men among the Jews, as in other nations, often cut off in their youth? Or was long life always a blessing? We know it was not. Old age is necessarily subjected to many infirmities of the mind as well as of the body. And the old age of *Solomon*, who had been so eminently distinguished by the oracle of God, tarnished all the glory of his former life and reign.

It hath been asserted by most of the ancient and modern Christian writers, and is acknowledged by WARBURTON, that *Moses*, who had been bred up in all the learning of the *Egyptians*, believed the immortality of the soul, and a future state of rewards and punishments. But he carefully concealed this doctrine from the people, in obedience, as may be supposed, to the express command of God : for, if it were not so, would not he have taught a doctrine which he could have applied with more efficacy to the establishment of his power and government, than all his other ordinances, or those various arts and stratagems, which, from time to time, he was obliged to make use of to keep the people in subjection?

IT IS DIFFICULT to pronounce with certainty against any Latin production, especially when the author has acquired a reputation for his skill in that language; and yet nothing is more common than to hear a little pedant, or a bare smatterer in the Latin tongue, criticise the works of an elegant scholar, and magisterially affirm that such and such expressions are not classical. I have even known some persons, who were very conversant in the Latin classics, which they had made their principal study, expose themselves by a

too hasty censure of this kind. In the
year 1738, I published MILTONIS EPIS-
TOLA ad POLLIONEM. As this was a
political satire, and nothing in the same
manner had been published before in this
country, it was universally read by those
who either understood, or pretended to
understand the language, and was frequently extolled or condemned according to the prejudice of party : there was
not a courtier, or a creature of the prime
minister's, who did not set himself up as
a profound critic, and censured the style
of a composition which perhaps he could
not read. However, I must confess there
were some men of learning who found
fault with the diction, and would not
allow the Latin to be pure and classical;
which sentence they pronounced either

against the conviction of their own judgment (a part which envy will often act),
or perhaps, which I rather suspect, for
want of a more intimate acquaintance
with the language. There were at that
time two gentlemen in London, HUME
CAMPBELL, the late Lord Register of
Scotland, and HOOKE, the author of the
Roman History, with whom I had always
lived in some degree of friendship : they
had both studied the ancient classics;
but doubting their own judgment, as
well as my sufficiency, they consulted
MAITTAIRE, and desired his opinion of
the MILTONIS EPISTOLA, in respect only to
the Latinity. MAITTAIRE marked eleven
expressions as unclassical. These were
communicated to me in a letter, which
my friends sent me to Oxford. The

same evening, by the return of the post,
I answered nine of MAITTAIRE's excep-
tions, and produced all my authorities
from *Virgil, Ovid,* and *Tibullus ;* and by
the post following I sent authorities for
the other two. I could not help re-
marking that Maittaire, some little time
before, had published new editions of
those poets, from whence I drew my authorities, and had added a very copious
index to every author : and in these
indexes were to be found most of the
phrases to which he had excepted in the
MILTONIS EPISTOLA.

When I published the oration, which
I pronounced at the opening of the RAD-
CLIFFE library, I was immediately attacked by one SQUIRE of *Cambridge,* who
hath since been greatly promoted in the

church, and is, I think, Clerk of the Closet to the Prince of Wales. He asserted that six or seven expressions in this speech are barbarous Latin, though they are all to be found in the best Latin authors, as *Terence, Tully, Cæsar, Sallust,* &c. He was particularly so unfortunate as to usher in his criticisms with condemning the phrase *fortiter & constanter sèntire,* and to spend three or four whole pages to prove that this is neither Latin nor sense: that is, that CICERO could neither write one nor the other; for this is CICERO's Latin, and not mine. See the third book of his *Tusculan Questions,* and his oration for SULLA.

The rest of this critic's answer consists in low scurrilities and personal abuse, such as may be always expected from

men of mean birth, who in whatever station of life they may happen to be placed,
even when they attain the highest digni-
ties, and live within the air of the court,
always.retain the language and manners
of their father's house.

Another person, from whom I received
the same rude and dirty treatment upon
the same occasion, was Dr. JOHN BUR-
TON, a fellow of Eton College; but he
had more discretion than SQUIRE. He
did not venture to criticise any particular
passages, but censured my speech by the
lump, and condemned the whole as bad
Latin; and to give the greater weight to
his criticism, he made no scruple to add
a false fact, roundly affirming, that I first
writ it in *English,* and then translated it
into Latin, as if he had stood by me

whilst I was writing. The rest of his work is a collection of all the foul and scurrilous names with which the Latin language could furnish him, which he hath liberally bestowed upon me, intermixed with many praises and compliments which he bestowed on himself. I answered this performance by translating all the abusive names which were given me, and the fine appellations which BURTON had assumed to himself; and I printed the whole catalogue on a large sheet of coarse paper, such as Grubstreet ballads are generally printed on, and delivered the impression, which was a very large one, to a scavenger, to be cried about the streets of Oxford, Windsor, and Eton. And in truth, this is the only proper answer that can be 'made to a work of this kind; for foul language and hard names, when a man does not deserve them, like an overcharged gun, will always recoil on the author.

CLODIUS ACCUSAT MOECHOS, &c. is a character which is to be found in every country. How often have I heard a sordid miser accuse his neighbour of avarice, and a prodigal spendthrift prescribe rules of economy! LEE, who is the proudest man, and the greatest hypocrite in *England*, preaches against pride and hypocrisy, and BURTON, whom I have mentioned above*, officiously concerns himself in the private affairs of every family

---

* Who, whilst I am writing this, hath published three sermons on the following text, THAT YE STUDY TO BE QUIET AND DO YOUR OWN BUSINESS.

to which he is admitted, at the same time neglecting his own business and his duty as a parish priest. In these sermons likewise, the preacher, who is rude, overbearing, and in every respect very ill-bred, enlarges with great vehemence on the duty of good manners, and decent and polite behaviour. *Non vides id manticæ*, &c. may perhaps be urged as some kind of apology for BURTON, and all others of the same cast and complexion, who are so vain and opinionative, that they are unable to espy any fault in themselves. But the hypocrite is sensible of the crime which he practises to deceive you, and knows he is masked, and for the same purpose as an highwayman who robs with a piece of black crape on his face.

Somnium Academici. I mounted with great velocity above the clouds, until I found myself in the middle region of the air. Here was a new world, which I soon perceived to be the seat of happy souls; who, after they shall have continued in it the space of 10,000 years, will be removed to a more glorious orb, and again, after some ages, to another, still ascending higher and higher, till after some millions of years they attain the last state of purification. Every scene which presented itself to my view filled me with delight, and I felt a pleasure which no man who treads on the earth is capable of enjoying or describing. Although there were myriads of inhabitants in this happy region, yet there were no wars or tumults, no quarrels or disputes, no disorder or confusion. For as here were no ranks, titles, or distinctions, but all were equal, and were sensible likewise that this equality must ever remain, so there was no place for pride or ambition, for envy or hatred, for poverty or riches, or for that mad zeal and enthusiasm, by which so many flourishing states and kingdoms of the earth have been totally ruined. Every soul I met with saluted me in a most courteous manner; and I knew at first sight not only some of my contemporaries, but many eminent persons, who are recorded both in ancient and modern history, and some who have been dead near 3000 years. The first I particularly remarked was Ovid, in a circle of the best and most learned poets of the AUGUSTAN

age, amongst whom I observed seven of
my countrymen, Chaucer, Spenser, Wal-
ler, Cowley, Walsh, Parnel and Gay: and
I saw at a small distance Swift, and Ar-
buthnot coming to join them. As I always
loved and admired Ovid for the elegancy
of his wit, and the sweetness of his manners, I addressed myself to him; he received me with great politeness, and we
presently entered into an easy and familiar
conversation. He acquainted me with
many curious anecdotes of the court of
Augustus, and some very remarkable oc-
currences of his own time, as well as
of the former ages of Rome, which no
historian hath mentioned; this led me to
inquire of him the cause of his banishment, which I told him was unknown to
the world at this day; at the same time

I acquainted him with the ridiculous conjectures of his commentators. He seemed a little surprised, and assured me that the day he went into banishment, the emperor's whole court, and all the citizens of *Rome*, knew the real cause of his disgrace, and he wondered that an affair which was so public at that time should not have been transmitted to posterity together with his works. He asked me whether I had ever considered with attention the following lines :

> *Cur aliquid vidi ? Cur noxia lumina feci ?*
> *Cur imprudenti cognita culpa mihi ?*
> *Inscius Actæon vidit sine veste Dianam :*
> *Præda fuit canibus non minus ille suis.*
> *Scilicet in superis etiam fortuna luenda est :*
> *Nec veniam læso numine casus habet.*

In this passage, says *Ovid*, I have plainly intimated that my disgrace was owing to something which I had inadvertently seen, and not to any crime. . I will tell you the story in a few words : I was acquainted with a lady of the court, whose name was CLODIA; she was descended from an old Patrician family, and was about thirty years of age. She had a good face, was well shaped, and did not want wit. Her behaviour was modest, and her reputation untouched. I was always pleased to be of her party, and she seemed to be very fond of my company. As I had leave to visit at all hours, it unfortunately happened, that, entering her apartment one morning very early, I found the old emperor with her, and in such an attitude, as convinced me that my female friend was not a *Lucretia*. I retired with great precipitation; but I feared that I was undone from that moment. The jealousy and vindictive temper of AUGUSTUS, and the rage of the lady in being thus discovered, soon pronounced my sentence. However, this punishment, which I so pitifully complained of in all my letters from *Tomos,* and which I then considered as the greatest calamity, really proved the most fortunate circumstance of my life; for during my exile I made many just and serious reflections, which I never allowed myself to make in my prosperity, which purified my passions, and at length disposed my mind to resign itself to the will of providence. I was extremely pleased with this account which OVID gave me of himself, and to be so particularly informed of the real cause of his banishment, which I resolved to publish the first opportunity, for the benefit of the learned world. Here, the Roman poet more attentively considering me, asked me, " whether I was dead?" I told him, " I was not: but I hoped, as I was old and infirm, this would soon be my fate, and that I should be destined to ascend again to those happy mansions, and frequently have the pleasure of finding myself in the same circle." This humane and gentle spirit encouraged me to ask him an hundred questions concerning *Rome*, and the state of literature in the *Augustan* age: and I concluded with requesting him to give me the real character of the emperor. " If I were capable," says *Ovid*, " of feeling any remorse or disquietude in these happy

regions, the flattering speeches which I
bestowed on the emperor would create
in my mind no small uneasiness. He
by no means deserved any part of that
veneration which was so universally paid
him. He was false, cruel, and inexora-
ble; and the bloody executions which he
ordered during his triumvirate, and the
great number of persons of quality and
distinguished merit whom he put to
death upon the slightest suspicion, after
he was sole emperor, were a sufficient
proof of his natural disposition, and must
stain his memory as long as his name
shall be remembered in the world. He
put his tutor and companion to death,
and with his own hands pulled out the
eyes of *Aulus Gellius* the prætor. He
was not softened by age, or moved by

the widow or orphan. You see that all my submissions, and the united interest of all my noble friends, could not prevail on him to grant me so small a favour as to change the place of my banishment; though he was conscious that I had been guilty of no crime. I doubt whether he had personal courage: it is certain he had no fortitude of mind; a thunderstorm would drive him into a vault, or into any dark hole where he thought the lightning could not reach him. He was a sordid lover of money: and although he could command the wealth of the whole world, he was never generous to men of honour, nor ever bestowed a princely reward on any person of great merit and learning. Virgil and Horace owed their fortunes to Mæcenas only:' The latter was content with a moderate estate, and as he knew Au- gustus perfectly well, he declined ac- cepting some lucrative offices which had been offered him; but which required his personal attendance on the emperor. To conclude the character of this man, he was every day guilty of some base and mean action, either to gratify his lust and avarice, or to discover the real sentiments of the Roman people*." When Ovid had done, I repeated *Scaliger*'s verses, in which he introduces our poet speaking to Augustus. Ovid seemed to be much pleased with the two last lines,

Cum te laudarem, tunc sum mentitus: ob unum hoc
     Exilii fuerat debita causa mihi.

* How were we degenerated when we made this man a God!

L ⸱ THE ART. OF SPEAKING IN PUBLIC seems ⸱to be little understood in this country, notwithstanding .the necessity of practising it so frequently in the se- nate, in the pulpit, and at the bar; and notwithstanding a good speaker. in any profession may always make his way to ⸳riches and honours : a pulpit orator can scarce fail of arriving to some eminent dignity in the church, and a lawyer, with the same talents, of obtaining some of ⸳those great offices annexed to his profes- sion. ⸱ Even in the practice of physic this talent will be found very useful : and I knew a physician, who, although he had a very moderate share of medical knowledge; and was little skilled in the learned languages, yet by the assistance of strong natural parts, with an happy and graceful manner of speaking land addressing his patients, acquired by his practice 3000*l.* a year. It is a matter therefore of astonishment to me, that the art of speaking is not more diligently cultivated in the British Islands, especially in the universities, where it ought to be studied with the greatest assiduity. To this neglect must be imputed that languid manner in which our clergy generally deliver their sermons; so that a discourse, which may be unexceptionable as to its doctrine or argument, or even its language, will be so far from exciting the devotion, or convincing the judgment of the congregation, that it will not command their attention. Cicero, in his beautiful treatise *De Oratore*, quotes an expression of *Roscius*, the celebrated comedian, *Caput artis est,* DECERE, which is a very significant word, and in truth means every thing by which the speaker may conciliate the esteem and affection, and acquire the applause of his audience. ACTION, to which *De-mosthenes* attributes the whole excellency of an orator, is comprehended in this expression. And here, in regard to ACTION, I will mention one thing, which I do not remember to have been remarked by any of our countrymen who have treated on this subject, that the speaker's action must be accommodated to the genius and manners of his country; for the same action which may please in one country, would not be suffered in another. I could name some eminent preachers, who were the admiration of all Paris,

and yet, on account of their action, would
have been ridiculed by an English congregation. And, moreover, I venture
on this occasion to affirm, that however
a player may be taught action, yet the
action of an orator must always be natural,
and the effect of those expressions by
which he is animated. My friends have
often assured me, that whenever I spoke
in the theatre, they were pleased with
my action: but I scarce knew when I
used it, and when I did not, and it was
always produced by what I felt within.

The young gentlemen who spoke verses
in the theatre when the Earl of Westmorland was installed Chancellor of the
University were taught their action by
SHERIDAN the player. But their action
was *outrée* and ungraceful. Now, be-

sides his action, the speaker should take care to be properly dressed, suitably to his age, his station, and his country. This is an instruction certainly included in the DECERE, and however insignificant it may be thought by some, is of no small advantage; more especially if the orator be a graceful person; which scarce ever fails to prejudice the audience in his favour*.

It is a great defect in the education of

---

* VALERIUS MAXIMUS mentions only three great Roman orators, C. GRACCHUS, CICERO, and HORTENSIUS. Of the last he remarks, Q. HORTENSIUS *plurimum in corporis decoro motu repositum credens, penè plus studii in eodem elaborando, quàm in ipsâ eloquentiâ affectandâ impendit.* And he adds, *Itaque constat* ÆSOPUM *et* ROSCIUM *ludicræ artis peritissimos viros, illo* (scil. HORTENSIO) *causas agente, in coronâ frequenter astitisse, ut foro petitos gestus in scenam referrent.*

our youth, in both the universities, that they do not sufficiently apply themselves to the study of their mother tongue. By this means it happens, that some very learned men and polite scholars are not able to express themselves, with propriety in common conversation, and that when they are discoursing on a subject which they understand perfectly well. I have been acquainted with * three persons only who spoke English with that elegance and propriety, that if all they said had been immediately committed to writing, any judge of the English language would have pronounced it an excellent and very

* ATTERBURY, the exiled Bishop of Rochester.
Dr. GOWER, Provost of Worcester College.
JOHNSON, the author of the English Dictionary, of the *Rambler,* &c.

beautiful style. And yet among the
French and *Italians* we meet with few
learned men who are not able to express
themselves with ease and elegance in
their own language; and if the same
freedom of speech were allowed in the
parliament of *Paris*, or senate of *Rome*,
which may be used in an English house
of commons, their orators would be more
numerous and eminent than we can boast
of. Observing this defect so universal
in the English nation, I have always advised the young gentlemen who were
under my care in the university, or with
whom I had any connexion or acquaintance (especially those who had parts,
and discovered an inclination to improve
themselves), to get by heart a page in one
of our English classics every morning, in

order to speak their own tongue with facility, and acquire a good style in writing. This method I once recommended to two brothers, young gentlemen of a noble family, who had been educated in Holland, and on their return to their own country could speak no other language 'than *French* or *Dutch*: they pursued my advice with such assiduity that they both became eminent speakers in parliament; and the eldest, who is now a peer, is esteemed inferior to no orator in the House of Lords. But after all, in my opinion, the art of oratory is not to be taught; it must be use and experience, and a man's own judgment, which must form the orator. There is sometimes a certain crisis in the public affairs, but oftener it is the nature of the government which excites youth to the study of eloquence. For fifty or sixty years before the ruin of the Roman republic there were more orators in Rome than are now to be found in all Europe; and yet I doubt whether in Rome, during the same period, there were as many learned men and profound scholars as are this day existing in the British Islands. Cicero affirms, that no man can be a PERFECT orator unless he be well skilled in all other arts and sciences; but his contemporaries seem to have been of a different opinion. The Roman senators generally thought they had a sufficient stock of learning if they were well skilled in the civil law, and understood the Greek language; and our parliament orators esteem themselves learned men,

N

if they are pretty well acquainted with the British constitution *. The most eminent lawyers in England, who by a constant use and practice must necessarily be ready speakers, know very little out of their own profession. For a century and an half we have had only two High Chancellors who could be called learned men, though many of them have been reputed excellent orators: and in our days, the man who enjoyed this great

---

* Amongst our numerous pleaders at the bar, I never heard any one argue methodically except my Lord MANSFIELD; which I ascribe to the logical lectures which he attended in the university. I have heard his predecessor RIDER, when be was Attorney-general, introduce all his arguments in such a confused and indistinct manner, that, although he said perhaps on the occasion all that could be said, yet I was not able to retain any part of his speech. He was in other respects a very ungraceful speaker.

office for twenty years, and during that
time dictated to the House of Peers, did
not learn Latin, as I am well assured,
until after he was made Lord Chancellor.
Sir ROBERT WALPOLE, who by his oratory raised himself from a small estate to
the height of power, and disposed of all
employments in the British dominions
for many years, had not any great stock
of learning. He was indeed not unskilled
in the classics ; some knowledge of those
authors he could not but retain, as he
had been formerly a fellow of a College
in Cambridge. I knew Sir William
Wyndham, who was allowed to be the
best and most graceful speaker in the
House of Commons for many years before he died, but he was not eminent in
any branch of literature. Mr. Pitt, who

has acquired such a great reputation for his eloquence, and a greater still for his administration, and the success which has attended it, has not much learning to boast of, unless it be some little acquaintance with the *Latin* classics. I could name several others, in both Houses of Parliament, who are busy speakers, and harangue on all occasions, who would be greatly puzzled in reading one of *Tully*'s orations. The truth is, that not only all philosophical studies, and the abstruser sciences, are of little use to our parliament orators, but even without a tincture of what we call polite literature, they are many of them able to talk themselves into esteem and good employments. Every age produces men (*very

* Two or three perhaps in a century. Such men

few indeed) who seem to be orators born, who not only without the aid of learning, but without use and exercise, which are so necessary to the formation of an orator, are endowed with a talent of speaking and replying readily and fluently. I have heard a speech from *Hodges*, the present town-clerk of London (who was bred a bookseller, and I am well assured is unskilled in any language but his own), which gave me more pleasure and satisfaction than I have received from the harangues of many of our celebrated orators, whether at the

may properly be called geniuses. Indeed our *methodists* and our enthusiasts of all denominations pretend to the gift of speaking; and it must be acknowledged they speak with great fluency and volubility: but it is always a flow of absurdities, blasphemy, and nonsense.

bar or in the senate. But, after all, a
man who has good parts and a good
judgment, and is ambitious of acquiring
the character of an orator, should form
himself after the ancient *Greek* and *Roman* models. He should study with great
application the orations of *Demosthenes*
and *Tully;* and he should always have
before him that most excellent work of
Tully's, *De Oratore*, wherein the precepts
are conveyed in such a pure and elegant
style, that the same are the best examples of what this great author proposes
to teach.

BUTLER, who was predecessor to the
present Bishop of Durham, being applied
to on some occasion for a charitable sub-
scription, asked his steward what money

he had in the house. The steward.informed him, " there was five hundred pounds." " Five hundred pounds!" said the Bishop : " what a shame for a Bishop to have such a sum .in his possession !" and ordered it all to be immediately given to the poor. That spirit of charity and benevolence which possessed this excellent man hath not appeared in any other part of the hierarchy since the beginning of, the present century. His successor, Dr. TREVOR, possessed of a large estate, besides the revenue of his rich bishopric, has a different turn of mind, but in common with many of his own order. To speak freely, I know nothing that has brought so great a reproach on the Church of England as the avarice and ambition of our bishops. CHANDLER,

Bishop of Durham, WILLIS, Bishop of Winchester, POTTER, Archbishop of Canterbury, GIBSON and SHERLOCK, Bishops of London, all died shamefully rich, some of them worth more than 100,000*l.* I must add to these my old antagonist GILBERT, predecessor to DRUMMOND, the present Archbishop of York. Some of these prelates were esteemed great divines (and I know they were learned men), but they could not be called good Christians. The great wealth which they heaped up, the fruits of their bishoprics, and which they left to enrich their families, was not their own; it was due to God, to the church, to their poor brethren. The history of the good *Samaritan,* which was so particularly explained by Christ himself to his disciples, ought to be a monitory to all their successors. I knew BURNETT, Bishop of Salisbury: he was a furious party-man, and easily imposed on by any lying spirit of his own faction; but he was a better pastor than any man who is now seated on the bishops' bench. Although he left a large family when he died, three sons and two daughters (if I rightly remember), yet he left them nothing more than their mother's fortune. He always declared, that he should think himself guilty of the greatest crime, if he were to raise fortunes for his children out of the revenue of his bishopric. It was no small misfortune to the cause of Christianity in this kingdom, that when we reformed from popery, our clergy were permitted to marry; from that

period their only care (which was natural, and must have been foreseen) was
to provide for their wives and children;
this the dignitaries, who had ample reve-
nues, could easily effect, with the loss,
however, of that respect and veneration
which they formerly received on account
of their hospitality* and numerous charities; but the greatest part of the inferior clergy were incapable of making
a provision for sons and daughters, and
soon left families of beggars in every
part of the kingdom. I do not inquire
whether chastity ought to be a requisite

---

* In the epistle which is read at the consecration
of our bishops, it is required of them amongst other
injunctions, that they *should be given to hospitality,
not given to filthy lucre, not covetous.* They likewise
solemnly promise *to assist the indigent, and all
strangers who are destitute of help.*

in those who are ordained to serve at the
altar (it certainly adds a grace and dignity to their function), but I cannot help
observing that our government makes
no difference between a bishop's wife and
his concubine; the wife has no place or
precedence, she does not share in her
husband's honours; although the creation
of a simple knight, whose honours, like
the bishop's, are for life only, gives a
rank and title to his wife. Moreover,
as an academician, and friend to the republic of letters, I have often wished
that the canons which forbid priests to
marry were still in force. To the celi-
bacy of the bishops we owe almost all
those noble foundations which are established in both our Universities; but
since the *Reformation*, we can boast of

few of the episcopal order as benefactors
to these seats of learning. The munifi-
cent donations of LAUD and SHELDON,
in the last century, will, indeed, ever be
remembered; but let it likewise be remembered, that these two prelates were
unmarried. Since the commencement
of the present century, I do not recollect
one of our Right Reverends who ought
to be recorded as an eminent patron of
learning, or learned men; but this will
not appear very wonderful, if we consider by what spirit they were dignified—
haud equidem spiritu sancto. And yet
in the consecration of these *conge d'elire*
bishops, they are said to be called to this
work by the Holy Ghost; and in their
answer to the archbishop, they seem to
affirm it of themselves.

QUUM A.POTENTISSIMIS illis viris, qui hujus Imperii res et rationes procurant, et gubernant, nulla præmia aut munera mihi petii, aut.fortasse unquam exoptavi, sanè quidem miror, quo malo fato natus tot inimicitias ego contraxerim, aut quæ sit causa, quamobrem viri nequissimi me præcipuè ex omnibus elegerint, in quem inveherentur; etiam quem accusarent graviorum criminum, et eorundem flagitiorum, quæ insani, quæ perjuri, atque ut uno verbo omnia dicam, quæ ipsi fecerunt et propè quotidiè faciunt; ut haud sciam profectò, an malus iste Deus horum hominum et calumniatorum omnium princeps et magister usque adeò maledicere et mentiri auderet.

This complaint .is occasioned by a

most infamous advertisement published
about' this time (Nov. 1761) in a news-
paper, on purpose to defame me, for no
other reason but because as a member
of the University I attended my brethren,
when with the whole body (our chancellor at their head) they waited on the
King with an address of congratulation
on his Majesty's marriage with the Prin-
cess of Mecklenburgh.   I have been re-
viled hitherto as a jacobite, and now I
am censured for going to court.   Of my
political principles, and the little concern
I have had in public transactions, I will
hereafter give a very candid account.
But here I only desire it may be observed, that my enemies of both parties
are the lowest of the people, who, besides
the scurrilous appellations which they

have constantly bestowed on me, have never scrupled to invent the most atrocious calumnies, and to charge me with crimes which my honest soul abhors. I have before taken notice of the illiberal criticisms of BURTON, and of the railing accusations brought against me by the execrable BLACOW, the famous dignified informer; I could not but expect from these men all that malice could forge and impudence would publish: but it never entered into my thoughts that a nonjuring clergyman, who values himself much upon the sanctity of his manners, and with whom I had once lived in some degree of friendship, should conspire with two or three villanous attorneys, who for a small bribe would swear away any man's life, to traduce

me by a public advertisement. However, I have now learned by my own experience, as also by the information of
some of my particular friends, that the
zeal of our non-juror grows more furious as he grows in years; and yet he
thinks every act not only lawful but
expedient which may serve to blacken a
man's character, who, he imagines, has
deserted his party, and been guilty of the
crime of going to court*. I don't know

---

* There is indeed a latent cause of this man's
enmity to me, besides the reason which he hath
given the public for his resentment. I have lately
been unfortunately engaged in a law-suit with one
JAMES BETTENHAM a printer, a sanctified member
of GORDON's congregation, but one of the greatest
knaves I have ever known. This man, who had
great obligations to me, and taken a great deal of
my money, endeavoured in settling a final account
to cheat me of 100*l*. In this attempt he was as-

whether he would be a martyr, but no man is a greater enthusiast in religion than he is in the Jacobite cause. *Hereditary right* and *passive obedience* are the chief articles of his creed. Talk to him of *public spirit* and the *amor patriæ*, 'tis a language which he does not understand; for he would be content to see the nation involved in a general ruin, and the extirpation of three or four millions of our people, if by that means the House of *Stuart* might be restored. And this is the doctrine which he teaches in the little congregation over which he presides as a pastor; where, while he boasts of the purity of his religion, and a

sisted and justified by his father confessor. The whole proceedings in this affair I propose to publish immediately.

steady adherence to his political system, he departs from every principle of humanity, and devotes his country to ruin. And in truth this personal abuse of me for no other reason but for an act of duty, which was required from me by the body corporate of which I am a member, was intended as a reflection on my superiors. Our zealot is enraged to see the extinction of faction, and such an harmony established amongst all orders and degrees as must necessarily prove our principal security. The nonjurors are now become a very insignificant and contemptible party. And although th Roman Catholics would certainly be ver glad to see their religion re-established in this country, yet there are few amongs them who would engage in any desperate measures for this purpose; and desperate they must be, when the odds are perhaps more than a thousand to one that an attempt of this kind does not succeed: which, as long as the present union of our people and their attachment to the sovereign subsist, may fairly be asserted. The means by which this union hath been effected must needs be a matter of inquiry amongst all foreign politicians, since our own observe it with a kind of wonder. A continual success in the conduct of our public affairs, and a series of victories, may justly be alleged as one of the principal causes of uniting many of those (however they have been distinguished by party) who are real lovers of their country. But this would not have reduced the Jacobite interest to the low condition in which we see it at present, unless some more powerful motives had influenced the leaders of that party to change their principles and desert a cause, to which they had so stedfastly adhered for so many years. As I can in some measure account for this defection, I shall probably render an acceptable service to many of my countrymen and satisfy the inquiries of posterity by publishing an anecdote, which I am now under no obligations to conceal, and which as the affairs of Britain are at present circumstanced, it would, in my opinion, be criminal in me to suppress.

SEPTEMBER   1750, I received a note from my Lady PRIMROSE, who desired to see me immediately. As soon as I

waited on her, she led me into her dress-ing-room, and presented me to ———*.
If I was surprised to find him there, I was still more astonished when he ac-quainted me with the motives which had induced him to hazard a journey to Eng-land at this juncture. The impatience of his friends who were in exile had formed a scheme which was impracticable ; but although it had been as feasible as they had represented it to him, yet no pre-paration had been made, nor was any thing ready to carry it into execution. He was soon convinced that he had been deceived, and therefore, after a stay in London of five days only, he returned to the place from whence he came. As I had some long conversa-

* The Pretender.

tions with him here, and for some years after held a constant correspondence with him, not indeed by letters but by messengers*, who were occasionally despatched to him; and as during this intercourse I informed myself of all particulars relating to him and of his whole conduct, both in public and private life, I am perhaps as well qualified as any man in England to draw a just character of him; and I impose this task on myself not only for the information of posterity, but for the sake of many worthy gentlemen whom I shall leave behind me, who are at present attached to his name, and who have formed their ideas

---

* These were not common couriers, but gentlemen of fortune, honour, and veracity, and on whose relations I could entirely depend.

of him from public report, but more particularly from those great actions which he performed in Scotland. As to his person, he is tall and well-made, but stoops a little, owing perhaps to the great fatigue which he underwent in his northern expedition. He has an handsome face and good eyes; (I think* his busts, which about this time were commonly sold in London, are more like him than any of his pictures which I have yet

---

* He came one evening to my lodgings and drank tea with me: my servant, after he was gone, said to me, " that he thought my new visitor very like Prince Charles." " Why," said I, " have you ever seen Prince Charles?" " No, sir," replied the fellow, " but this gentleman, whoever he may be, exactly resembles the busts which are sold in Red-lion-street, and are said to be the busts of Prince Charles." The truth is, these busts were taken in plaster of Paris from his face.

seen ;) but in a polite company he would not pass for a genteel man.   He hath a quick apprehension, and speaks *French, Italian,* and *English,* the last with a little of a foreign accent.   As to the rest, very little care seems to have been taken of his education.   He had not made the belles lettres or any of the finer arts his study, which surprised me much, considering his preceptors, and the noble opportunities he must have always had in that nursery * of all the elegant and liberal arts and science.   But I was

* ROME. His governor was a protestant, and I am apt to believe purposedly neglected his education, of which it is surmised he made a merit to the English ministry; for he was always supposed to be their pensioner. The Chevalier Ramsay, the author of Cyrus, was Prince Charles's preceptor for about a year; but a court faction removed him.

still more astonished, when I found him unacquainted with the history and constitution of *England*, in which he ought to have been very early instructed. I never heard him express any noble or benevolent sentiments, the certain indications of a great soul and a good heart; or discover any sorrow or compassion for the misfortunes of so many worthy men who had suffered in his cause*. But the most odious part of his character is his love of money, a vice which I do not

* As to his religion, he is certainly free from all bigotry and superstition, and would readily conform to the religion of the country. With the catholics he is a catholic; with the protestants he is a protestant; and, to convince the latter of his sincerity, he often carried an English Common Prayer-book in his pocket: and sent to Gordon (whom I have mentioned before), a nonjuring clergyman, to christen the first child he had by Mrs. W.

remember to have been imputed by our historians to any of his ancestors, and is the certain index of a base and little mind. I know it may be urged in his vindication, that a prince in exile ought to be an economist. And so he ought; but nevertheless his purse should be always open, as long as there is any thing in it to relieve the necessities of his friends and adherents. King Charles the second, during his banishment, would have shared the last pistole in his pocket with his little family. But I have known this gentleman with two thousand Louis-d'ors in his strong box pretend he was in great distress, and borrow money from a lady in Paris, who was not in affluent circumstances. His most faithful ser-vants, who had closely attended him in

all his difficulties, were ill rewarded.
Two Frenchmen, who had left every
thing to follow his fortune, who had been
sent as couriers through half Europe,
and executed their commissions with
great punctuality and exactness, were
suddenly discharged without any faults
imputed to them, or any recompense for
their past service. To this spirit of avarice may be added his insolent manner
of treating his immediate dependants,
very unbecoming a great prince, and a
sure prognostic of what might be expected from him if ever he acquired
sovereign power. Sir J. HARRINGTON *,

---

* Sir J. HARRINGTON remained in banishment till
the accession of the present King George III. No
man is better acquainted with the private history and
character of Prince Charles, and, if ever he reads
what I have here written, I am confident that he
will readily vouch the truth of my narrative.

and *Col. GORING, who suffered themselves to be imprisoned with him, rather
than desert him, when the rest of his
family and attendants fled, were afterwards obliged to quit his service on account of his illiberal behaviour. But
there is one part of his character, which
I must particularly insist on, since it
occasioned the defection of the most
powerful of his friends and adherents in
England, and by some concurring acci-
dents totally blasted all his hopes and
pretensions. When he was in Scotland,
he had a mistress, whose name is Walk-

---

* GORING, upon quitting his service, was recommended by my Lord MARSHAL to the King of Prussia,
who immediately gave him a command in his army,
equal to his pretensions. GORING died soon after,
and his loss was greatly lamented by his PRUSSIAN
Majesty, who honoured him with a character in a
letter to my Lord MARSHAL.

enshaw, and whose sister was at that time, and is still housekeeper at Leicester House. Some years after he was released from his prison, and conducted out of France, he sent for this girl, who soon acquired such a dominion over him, that she was acquainted with all his schemes, and trusted with his most secret correspondence. As soon as this was known in England, all those persons of distinction, who were attached to him, were greatly alarmed; they imagined that this wench had been placed in his family by the English ministers; and, considering her sister's situation, they seemed to have some ground for their suspicion; wherefore they despatched a gentleman to *Paris*, where the Prince then was, who had instructions to insist that Mrs. Walkenshaw should be removed to a convent for a certain term; but her gallant absolutely refused to comply with this demand; and although Mr. M'Namara, the gentleman who was sent to him, who has a natural eloquence, and an excellent understanding, urged the most cogent reasons, and used all the arts of persuasion to induce him to part with his mistress, and even proceeded so far as to assure him, according to his instructions, that an immediate interruption of all correspondence with his most powerful friends in England, and in short that the ruin of his interest, which was now daily increasing, would be the infallible consequence of his refusal; yet he continued inflexible, and all M'Namara's intreaties and remonstrances were ineffectual. M'Namara staid in Paris some days beyond the time prescribed him, endeavouring to reason the Prince into a better temper; but finding him obstinately persevere in his first answer, he took his leave with concern and indignation, saying, as he passed out, " what has your family done, Sir, thus to draw down the vengeance of Heaven on every branch of it through so many ages?" It is worthy of remark, that in all the conferences which M'Namara had with the Prince on this occasion, the latter declared, that it was not a violent passion, or indeed any particular regard*,

* I believe he spoke truth when he declared he had no esteem for his northern mistress, although she has been his companion for so many years. She had no elegance of manners: and as they had both

which attached him to Mrs. Walkenshaw,
and that he could see her removed from
him without any concern; but he would
not receive directions in respect to his
private conduct from any man alive.
When M'Namara returned to London,
and reported the Prince's answer to the
gentlemen* who had employed him, they

contracted an odious habit of drinking, so they exposed themselves very frequently, not only to their
own family, but to all their neighbours. They often
quarreled and sometimes fought: they were some
of these drunken scenes which, probably, occasioned
the report of his madness.

* These were all men of fortune and distinction,
and many of them persons of the first quality, who
attached themselves to ——— as to a person who,
they imagined, might be made the instrument of
saving their country. They were sensible, that by
WALPOLE's administration the English government
was become a system of corruption, and that WAL-
POLE's successors, who pursued his plan without any
of his abilities, had reduced us to such a deplorable

were astonished and confounded. However, they soon resolved on the measures
which they were to pursue for the future,
and determined no longer to serve a man
who could not be persuaded to serve
himself, and chose rather to endanger
the lives of his best and most faithful
friends, than part with an harlot, whom,
as he often declared, he neither loved
nor esteemed. If ever that old adage
Quos Jupiter vult perdere, &c. could be
properly applied to any person, whom
could it so well fit as the gentleman of
whom I have been speaking? for it is

situation, that our commercial interest was sinking,
our colonies in danger of being lost, and Great
Britain, which, if her powers were properly * ex-
erted, was able to give laws to other nations, was
become the contempt of all *Europe*.

* As they were afterwards in Mr. PITT's administration.

difficult by any other means to account for such a sudden infatuation. * He was, indeed, soon afterwards made sensible of his misconduct, when it was too late to repair it: for from this era may truly be dated the ruin of his cause; which, for the future, can only subsist in the

---

* He was soon made acquainted with the defection which immediately followed upon the report of his answer. He endeavoured to excuse himself by blaming the gentleman who had been sent to him; he pretended the message had not been properly delivered, that he had been treated rudely and insolently, &c. But this was not the case. Mr. M'Namara addressed him in the most respectful manner, and though he spoke firmly, as he knew the consequence of the Prince's refusal, yet he could not have treated him with more deference if he had been on the throne. The Prince's accusation of M'Namara was very unjust, as well as ungrateful, for M'Namara had been often with him, and had served him with great zeal and fidelity on many important occasions, both at home and abroad.

N—n—ing congregations, which are generally formed of the meanest people,
from whom no danger to the present
government need ever be apprehended.
Before I close this article, I must observe, that during this transaction, my
Lord M—— was at *Paris* in the
quality of Envoy from the K—— of
P——; M'Namara had directions to
acquaint him with his commission: my
Lord M—— not in the least doubting the Prince's compliance with the request of his friends in England, determined to quit the K—— of P——'s service as soon as his embassy was finished,
and go into the Prince's family. This
would have been a very fortunate circumstance to the Prince on all accounts,
but more especially as nothing could be

more agreeable to all those persons of figure and distinction, who were at that time so deeply engaged in his cause; for there was not one of all that number who would not have reposed an entire confidence in the honour and discretion of my Lord M————. But how was this gentleman amazed, when he perceived the Prince's obstinacy and imprudence? who was resolved, by a strange fatality, to alienate the affections of his best friends, and put an absolute barrier to all his own hopes. From this time my Lord M———— would never concern himself in this cause; but prudently embraced the opportunity, through the K—— of P——'s interest, of reconciling himself to the *English* government.

Since I wrote this article, I have met

with a pamphlet lately published (1762)
in French, entitled, *Testament Politique
du Maréchal Duc de Belleisle.* The
author of this work is said to be the
present writer of the Brussels Gazette:
he pretends to know, that when the
French had resolved on the expedition
against Minorca, the command of their
troops was offered to Prince Charles,
which he refused, complaining of his
imprisonment in the Castle of *Vincennes*,
et finit par me dire (says Mr. Belleisle)
que les Anglois lui rendroient justice,
s'ils le jugeoient à propos; mais qu'il ne
vouloit plus être leur *épouvantail.* I can
scarce believe the command of this
expedition was ever offered to Prince
Charles; but if it were, I can easily believe that his answer was such as this

author has reported; for he had often
declared to his friends, after the ill treatment which he had received from the
Court of *France*, that he never would
accept of any offers which that court
might hereafter make him, which never
had any real intention to serve him, but
only to use him occasionally as their instrument, and to sacrifice him to their
own interest. He knew enough of the
history of his family to have learnt this
truth, and he had on two or three occasions experienced it in himself.

SOMNIUM ACADEMICI ALTERUM. Mihi
denuo sit propitia Mnemosyne animum
revocanti ad carum rerum memoriam,
quibus ipse interfui, quum nocte hesternâ
nescio quomodo, peregrè abirem, et in

iis errarem regionibus, quæ solâ Mor-
phei ditione gubernantur : Ubi Deus ille
ita aptè formas personasque omnes sibi
induit, aliisque imponit, uti re verâ eos
esse, qui simulantur, Deos atque homines
putemus. Et mehercule haud ferè quis-
quam mortalium aut immortalium, præter - Pseudo-Amphytrionem et Sosiam
suum, histrioniam uspiam gentium visus
est exquisitius facere. Vellem etiam
mihi propitias esse Musas et Apollinem,
non multum aut nihil omninò, quod poeta-
rum celeberrimorum ritu, iis molestus
essem, et centum ora linguasque aut ali-
quid magnum postularem. Sed utinam
sic agerem, ut mihi potestatem Musæ
concedant transformandi ineptos quos-
dam scriptores aliosque viros improbos
et academiæ nostræ inimicissimos, in

picas .aut porcos ; útque sagittifer ille
* * * * * *. certa spicula aut tela acutiora
ex pharetrâ aut armamentario suo de-
prompta mihi donet, quò aliquando ar-
ceam. a sedibus hisce ornatissimis et libertatis æde magnam istam et perjuram
delatorum et ardelionum nationem. Quod
ad hodiernam disputationem attinet, satis
mihi cautum fuisse spero, quòd Latiali
sermone usus sum,. quem quidem neque-
unt exponere, fortasse ne quidem legere
* BLACONES isti, qui optimatibus nostris

---

* BLACONES apud Anglos sunt infames delatores,
gigantum filii; quos naturâ malevolos spes præmii
induxit in summum scelus: qui quum castos et in-
tegerrimos viros accusare soleant, omnia confingunt,
et non modò perjuria sua vendunt, verum etiam alios
impellunt ad pejerandum. Nomen sumunt a BLACOW
quodam sacerdote, qui ob nefarias suas delationes
donatus est canonicatu Vindsoriensi a regni præfecto
D. de N. Quanta heu, heu, illo tempore fuerunt sce-
lerum præmia !

se magnificè jactant, ostentantque, quosque scio jam pollicituros se quàm sagacissimè odorari posse quid et ipse sentiam, et tota hæc fabula velit.

Quum Junii Calendis MDCCLX iter ad provinciam Cantii facerem et jam advesperasceret, in diversorio celebri et lauto decrevi requiescere. Ibi in tres incidi ex familiaribus meis, viros nobiles, eruditos, facetos; qui omni suâ comitate me complexi, ad coenam quam apparari jusserant, quàm humanissimè invitabant. Inter coenandum me evocavit rusticus quidam facie rubicundâ, latis humeris, cruribus ocreatis, et russeis vestibus indutus, qui dexteram meam prehendens digito auriculari aptavit ferreum annulum, inquiens, In hoc salus: dumque rogo, Quid istuc verbi est? fugit, evanuit.

Redeo ad cœnam narro omnia: vident
amici, requiruntque, ut annulum inspi-
ciant, quem quum ter et amplius de digito conatus sum detrahere, neque id
summâ vi efficere potui, subita superstitio
mentem meam occupavit, quasi ab hôc
conatu quodam numine repulsus essem.
Atque hôc prodigio ita commoveor (quod
verò adjuvit hilaritatem comitum meorum) ut ne verbum quidem adjicere possem, et nescio quid triste expectarem.
Itaque, cùm opportunum erat tempus,
cubitum discessi, et sive ex mœstitiâ sive
ex lassitudine arctius dormivi, neque pos-
tero die nisi post horam nonam exper-
rectus sum. Interea autem quæ pericula
subii! quæ maria transii! quas regiones
peragravi! quos homines, quos deos adii,
cognovi! Vix enim obrepserat somnus,

quum in mari Atlantico navigabam velis plenissimis. Puppis erat ingens, valida, deaurata, tam pedestribus quàm navalibus copiis instructa. Miratus sortem meam dum ex nautis quærere coepi, cujus esset navigium, et quo tenderet, in me torvè intuens præfectus, navis peregrinâ veste indutum, rogavit, Qui, et unde ipse essem, et cujus ope, et quo animo navem conscenderem omninò nullo diplomate munitus. Cumque obstupui, nec quid responderem, inveni, me quasi curiosum speculatorem cujus capite navis deberet, lustrari, in mare ejici jussit. Illico me aggrediuntur tres quatuorve ex nautis robustioribus, et frustrà clamantem me innoxium esse nimis inhumaniter ejiciunt. At quæ mira jam in mari sunt facta cum meo magno commodo: mihi adfuit ca-.

denti ipse Triton, meque in viciniâ mor-
tis quàm humanissimè accepit, et in curru
suo, affabre quidem facto, ea conchâ
splendidissimâ, collocavit.   Currum tra-
hebant equi marini, quorum vim ac cele-
ritatem præcipuè sum admiratus : nabant
enim seu volitabant aurâ ocyus.   Neque
verò Jonas in cetis ventre latitans, neque
Arion delphino insidens, aut Europa tauri
dorso tutius navigabant.   Interèa me
docuit Triton de ferrei annuli virtute et
potentia, deinde quo mei causâ dirigeret
iter ad insulam scilicet Neptuno sacram
in primis, nobile solum, et cui me credere
possem, si literarum colerem studia, aut
siquid negotiationis genus mihi placeret.
Dum benignitati Dei marini gratias ago,
ad littus deferimur.   Protinus ego in
terram desilio, et Triton ter et amplius

mihi vale dicens in mare revertitur. Ut
me adspexerunt rustici quidam in littore
spatiantes, barbaro suo more cuncti pro-
currunt, mea omnia, quasi certissimam
prædam sibi proponentes. Dumque in
me impetum facere conantur, subitò
prope astant immobiles deinde, tanquam
terrore panico concitati, terga vertunt,
et aufugiunt. Haud procul vidi mediocre
diversorium, ubi nautæ et piscatores totos
dies potabant. Hic cibo meroque postquam corpus curavi, curru quadrigarum
conductitio vectus sum ad urbem, quam
Argentariam vocant, insulæ caput. Ut
urbem intravi, cernere erat ad dextram
templum magnificentissimum, ornatissi-
mum. E curru descendi curiosus spec-
tator, et servis equisque præmissis ad
templi porticum accessi. In eo placidè

ambulantem aspicio senem quendam vultu læto et fiorido, purpurea veste indutum. Saluto hominem quasi peregre adveniens, sciscitorque cujus hæc sit ædes splendidissima, et cui Deo dicata. O hospes, inquit purpuratus, hæc est ædes Divi Augusti Gondiberti, qui nuper in coelum abiit. Si quæris, Quid ille hominis fuerit, aut quid meritus sit, ut tanti habitet, en ejus effigiem. Hæc locutus sinistram prehendit, meque in templum duxit, ubi in medio positam statuam Gondiberti inauratam vidi, cujus in basi hoc elogium erat incisum:

Sacrum. Esto.

Divo. Augusto. Gondiberto. Secundo.

Argentariae. Regi. Sapientissimo.

Imperatori. Fortissimo. Invictissimo. Clementissimo.

Germanico. Asiatico. Africano. Americano.

Pio. Facili. Jucundo. Magnanimo.

Cultori. Optimarum. Artium. Assiduo.
Patrono. Literatorum. Omnium. Munificentissimo.
Omnibus. Amicissimo.
Omnibus. Dilectissimo.
Patriae. et. Libertatis. Parenti.
Et. Seculi. Sui. Decori. et. Ornamento.

Jamque paratus et ipse eram GONDI-
BERTI memoriam venerari, cùm in ædem
introiit Stoicus quidam calvus, gravis,
severus, virgulam divinam in manu ges-
tans; qui in me intuens, Cave, inquit,
hospes, temerè credas speciosæ huic
inscriptioni. Divus sit, necne, defunc-
tus, sanè nescio : at cujusmodi fuerit
homo, probè scio, et faciam, ut tu sciàs.
Tunc virgulâ feriens statuæ basin, de
improviso immutatum est et evanuit
magnificum istud elogium, et hoc alterum
pro eo est substitutum.

Hic situs est,
Qui dictis et incessu semper patuit
MILES GLORIOSUS ;
Sed rei militaris scientiæ æquè ac artium liberalium
Omnino omnium ignarus,
Nescitur quo malo fato, fuit eheu! potentissimus ;
Sed injustus, superbus, sordidus, inhumanus.
Laudum cupidissimus
Se Laude summâ dignum existimavit.
At vixit quamvis annos plus septuaginta,
Haud quidquam unquam fecit facinus laudabile.
Nemini cuiquam amatus
Neminem quemquam, præter seipsum, amavit,
Ne quidem liberos, aut nepotes.
Sexcenta millia auri pondo corrasit,
Non hostes, sed suos opprimendo, & spoliando.
Nam ardenti fuit avaritiâ,
Et auri usque ad furorem appetens;
Quòd unum vigilans, somnians
Cogitabat, quærebat, admirabatur, venerabatur.
Et mehercule si Midas rex fuisset,
Nunquam suùm damnâsset votum
Sed, sacculis inhians, lætus periisset
Aurum creando.

Paulo inferius hoc præterea in eodem

basi, sed literis majusculis inscriptum notavi:

Qui veritatem amas, et quaeris,
En tibi Elogium sanè verissimum!
Tu verò,
Cui MILITI huic GLORIOSO concessum est
Succedere,
Tui, et patriae causâ sis ei quam dissimillimus!
Teque memineris
Neque Deum esse, neque lupum,
Sed Hominem!

Iterum iterumque hoc epigramma oculis intentis contemplatus sum, et vix mihi persuasum est ita ea prorsus esse quæ vidi, legi, et relegi: usque adeo magica hæc transmutatio mihi admirationem movit. Jamque circumspiciens quærebam senem purpuratum, qui primum in hanc ædem me invitabat. Stoicus verò, frustra, inquit, purpuratum quæris. Ut enim introii, ille se ex æde proripuit,

Q

conspectum meum veritus, et hujus vir-
gulæ virtutem; quæ falsas historias, et
mendacia impudentiora levi tactu obli-
terat et abradit, et vanas esse, uti cernis,
omnes eas prædicationes, quæ GONDI-
BERTUM nostrum in deorum numerum
retulere.

CONTINUATIO ET SERIES RERUM SIVE
FABULARUM SOMNIO ACADEMICI ANNEC-
TENDA. Quid autem isthuc, inquam,
obsecro, est negotii, aut cujusce modi
homo is est, qui me quàm familiariter in
hoc fanum invitavit, quique, ut te con-
spicatus est, virgulam tuam divinam in
manu gestantem, repentè aufugit. Iste,
ait Stoicus, vir est magni nominis. Sub
regno Gondiberti II^{di}. regni fuit præfectus et nisi a gubernaculis reipublicæ

tandem dejectus fuisset, maximum mehercule non modo ab hostium vi, sed ab
universo naufragio nobis esset pericu-
lum. Haud dissimilis est ei SUECICO
senatori et præfecto, quem in notis ad
PERILLÆ EPISTOLAM penicillo tuo scitè
pinxisti. Nunc verò, septuagenarius
quamvis, sortis suæ impatiens, et vitâ
privatâ et quietâ minimè contentus novas
res molitur, et qui patriæ semper pessimè
consuluit, nunc iterùm per bonorum
omnium proscriptiones ad regni præfec-
turam aspirat. Inter hæc, quæ de Argentariæ statu me docebat Stoicus, in
templum introiit pontifex maximus pur-
purâ et auro nitens, magnâ procerum
coccineis vestibus indutorum comitante
caterva; qui ut consedère (iis enim omnibus subsellia destinabantur) aream

templi et porticum implebant inferioris ordinis cives. Ego invitatus a templi custodibus inter hospites et peregrinos, qui, ex more civitatis humanissime, accipiebantur, satis commodè sedebam, cumque, quid agendum esset, sciscitabar, in rostrum ascendit senex octogenarius, calvus, decrepitus, quem, acclamante cœtu, ita locutum fuisse benè memini. Orationem hodie habiturus iis haud dissimilis videor, qui quum longinquum iter facere cogitant, idque negotia quædam nec opinata de die in diem impedierint, amicos et propinquos iterum arcessere, iterum amplexari, et quibus jam novò valedixerunt, iterum valedicere solent. At verò in hunc locum me invitum ascendisse fateor; quippe sentio, quàm animi vires perinde atque corporis

me deficiant, et vereor ut eas, quas sus-
cepi partes implere, aut quippiam cœtu
hoc illustrissimo dignum proferre possim.
Quid autem facerem! mihi hoc mandavit
officium   ita ut neque de-
precationi esset locus, neque ætatis ex-
cusatione liceret uti. Quamobrem vos
oro,   ut extremo huic sermoni meo
veniam detis: Veniam a vobis pro laude
peto. Cætera quidem petenda sunt a
libero illo spiritu, qui in difficillimo meo
tempore semper mihi. adfuit, et nunc
adest; qui neque potentissimorum hominum gratiam quærit, neque novam opti-
matum factionem colit, neque populi
furorem metuit, neque quid veri dicere
non audet pro patriâ, pro   pro
salute communi causam dicturus. Cùm
per. annos plus quadraginta regni præ-

fecti, sed homines iniquissimi hanc civi-
tatem, hanc Musarum domum, opprimere
sunt aggressi, quam exterminandam vel-
lent, eam hodie non modò salvam sed
florentem videmus: utque auspicatius
sermonem meum instituam, IN ÆTER-
NUM FLOREAT! Cui verò fortunam nos-
tram, et hodiernam felicitatem debeamus,
neminem fugit. Ille enim princeps sere-
nissimus, atque idem hostis et victor
æquissimus, postquam christiano orbi pacem dederat, nos et patriis juribus, et
perfectâ libertate, et otio hoc literato
voluit et jussit frui. Ecquis autem pu-
taret, ecquis non doleret repertos esse
ex incolis nostris, qui res prosperas et
fortunatum hunc reipublicæ statum minimè possint pati? Nonne videtur an-
tiqua ea hujus insulæ ferocitas et bar-

baries rediisse, et quorumdam civium
mores penitùs imbuisse, qui bellum,
cædes et rapinas, concordiæ tranquilli‑
tati, et saluti communi anteferendas esse
censeant? A quo fonte derivata sint
hæc mala sub regno principis mitissimi
justissimique, quod quidem posteris quasi
monstri simile videbitur, Vos   non
ignoratis. En enim quasi altera conju‑
ratio Catilinaria! Sunt ex ipsis sena‑
tóribus, quos trahit ambitio, sunt quos
urget avarities, sunt quos impellit egestas,
omnes pessimo ingenio usos. Hi impri‑
mis libertatem publicam, quæ in rebus
omnibus moderationem servare debet,
esse asserunt quodcunque sibi (at sibi
solis) facere libeat. Hinc regis acta et
senatûs consulta palam calumniantur, et
criminantur. Hinc imperitum vulgus et

Argentariæ faecem aut verborum præ-
stigiis capiunt, aut largitionibus corrum-
punt. .. Hinc impudentissimè postulant
per oratorem suum, ut summa rerum et
negotiorum omnium potestas sibi suisque
tradatur, et nihil regi præter nomen inane
maneat. Hinc denique antiquæ et semper venerandæ gentis religioni, atque
(O infandum !) ipsi Deo maledicere
audent. Supervacaneum esset vos hor-
tari (quorum virtutes et prudentia ad-
hortationes minimè desiderant) ut nequis vestrûm huic factioni accedat, aut
cum hisce seditionis auctoribus amicitiâ
aut hospitio conjungatur: at mehercule
diligenter caveri oportet, ut nequis vir
bonus specie recti decipiatur; quippe
adversarii nostri, dum res novas moliun-
tur, et unum hoc cogitant, quo modo

regem et rempublicam possint opprimere,
de fide et virtute suâ gloriantur, seque
imprimis studere fingunt, ut populi libertatem, et jura legesque nostras tueantur.
Vos autem, Juvenes   præcipuè
cautos esse velim, nè adolescentia vestra,
quæ minimè est suspicax, horum hominum fallaciis et simulationibus circum-
veniatur.   Opto & spero, ut bonam eam
indolem, integritatem et ingenium, quæ
hodie hujus loci præfectis vos commend-
ant, in omni vitâ, inque negotiis cum do-
mesticis tum publicis semper obtineatis.
Sunt ex vobis qui in Senatum magnum
cooptentur; sunt qui fortasse sint pri-
mores regni: quæ fortuna si vobis con-
tigerit, tum verò maxime dignitati et
existimationi vestræ consulere oportebit:
tum præterea omnibus constet eum vobis

insitum esse amorem patriæ et moderationem animi, ut neque mali quæstûs
neque malæ ambitionis causâ vos reipublicæ unquam defuturi sitis. Sæpè ego
miratus sum (ut antèa dixi) ex popu-
laribus nostris inveniri, qui bellum ini-
quum quam pacem malunt honestissi-
mam, at mehercule multo magis miror et
indignor homines hosce gloriosos cives
esse ignavissimos et luxu diffluentes, qui
haud unquam rebus suis consulunt, quò
scilicet omnia turbent et pessimè de re-
publicâ mereantur, nisi inter cœnandum
et potandum. Quid verò si in eorum
mores et animum propiùs inspiceres?
nonne statim exclamares, Quam turpe
foedus! quàm perversa conjunctio! quam
discors concordia! Siquidem ex hujus
factionis principibus quamvis neminem

quemquam cognoveris, quin is ceteros
omnes, socios scilicet suos et convivas
quotidianos prorsùs contemnat et odio
habeat; quodcunque tamen quis sentiat
contra rempublicam, idem omnes sen-
tiunt. Huic conventui factioso sese so-
cium et consiliarium addidit Argentariæ
prætor vir sordidissimus. Is, ut non
nullius pretii inter suos habeatur, totius
Senatus auctoritatem, qui uno ore bonis
quibusdam civibus ob merita in rempublicam gratias agendas esse decreverat, in
curiâ negotiatorum, qua est impudentia,
voce suâ damnare haud dubitavit. O
quam fortunata esset respublica si pauci
ex sceleratissimis hisce senatoribus aliquò
in exteras regiones possent extrudi! Sed,
quia libertatem semper in ore habent,
quò machinationes suas et spem domina-

tionis occultius celare queant, et urbanæ
plebis clamoribus, et complurium civium,
qui corum consiliis favent, sententiis
muniti jus publicum violari quererentur,
siquid gravius de flagitiis suis esset ani-
madvertendum, idcirco rex mitissimus
injurias maximas & contumelias maluit
pati.   *   *   *   *   *   *

Quæ ultra mihi acciderunt, dum apud
ARGENTARIAM commoror, non est hodie
tutus narrandi locus. Posthæc videro,
an ea satis commodè possint dici.

OBLITUSQUE MEORUM, OBLIVISCENDUS
ET ILLIS, is the sincere desire of many
melancholy heads which are to be found
in the British dominions; and therefore I have often wished, that when we
reformed from popery a few convents

had been exempted from the general pillage, in which men of severe morals, or of a melancholy cast and turn of mind, might have found a retreat. But I have observed, what is perhaps peculiar to this island, that there are men wholly free from the spleen, or a lowness of spirits, in good health and good circumstances, and only actuated by some whimsical considerations, seek a retreat where they may forget their friends and relations, and be forgotten by them. About the year 1706, I knew one Mr. Howe, a sensible well-natured man, possessed of an estate of 700*l.* or 800*l.* per annum: he married a young lady of a good family in the west of England, her maiden name was Mallet; she was agreeable in her person and manners, and proved a very good wife. Seven or eight years after they had been married, he rose one morning very early, and told his wife he was obliged to go to the Tower to transact some particular business : the same day, at noon, his wife received a note from him, in which he informed her that he was under a necessity of going to Holland, and should probably be absent three weeks or a month. He was absent from her seventeen years, during which time she neither heard from him, or of him. The evening before he returned, whilst she was at supper, and with her some of her friends and relations, particularly one Dr. ROSE*, a physician, who had married her sister,

---

* I was very well acquainted with Dr. ROSE; he was of a French family. I often met him at King's Coffee-house, near Golden-square, and he frequently entertained me with this remarkable story,.

a billet, without any name subscribed, was delivered to her, in which the writer requested the favour of her to give him a meeting the next evening in the Bird-cage Walk, in St. James's Park. When she had read her billet, she tossed it to Dr. ROSE, and laughing, "You see, brother," said she, "as old as I am, I have got a gallant." ROSE, who perused the note with more attention, declared it to be Mr. HOWE's hand-writing: this surprised all the company, and so much affected Mrs. HOWE, that she fainted away; however, she soon recovered, when it was agreed that Dr. ROSE and his wife, with the other gentlemen and ladies who were then at supper, should attend Mrs. HOWE the next evening to the Bird-cage Walk: they had not been there more than five or six minutes, when Mr. HOWE came to them, and after saluting his friends, and embracing his wife, walked home with her, and they lived together in great harmony from that time to the day of his death.   But the most curious part of my tale remains to be related. * When HOWE left his wife, they lived in a house in Jermyn-street, near St. James's church ; he went no farther than to a little street in Westminster, where he took a room, for which he paid five or six shillings a week, and changing his

---

* LONDON is the only place in all Europe where a man can find a secure retreat, or remain, if he pleases, many years unknown. If he pays constantly for his lodging, for his provisions, and for whatsoever else he wants, nobody will ask a question concerning him, or inquire whence he comes, whither he goes, &c.

name, and disguising himself by wearing a black wig (for he was a fair man), he remained in this habitation during the whole time of his absence. He had had two children by his wife when he departed from her, who were both living at that time : but they both died young in a few years after. However, during their lives, the second or third year after their father disappeared, Mrs. Howe was obliged to apply for an act of parliament to procure a proper settlement of her husband's estate, and a provision for herself out of it during his absence, as it was uncertain whether he was alive or dead: this act he suffered to be solicited and passed, and enjoyed the pleasure of reading the progress of it in the votes, in a little coffee-house, near his lodging, which he frequented. Upon his quitting his house and family in the manner I have mentioned, Mrs. Howe at first imagined, as she could not conceive any other cause for such an abrupt elopement, that he had contracted a large debt unknown to her, and by that means involved himself in difficulties which he could not easily surmount; and for some days she lived in continual apprehensions of demands from creditors, of seizures, executions, &c. But nothing of this kind happened; on the contrary, he did not only leave his estate quite free and unencumbered, but he paid the bills of every tradesman with whom he had any dealings; and upon examining his papers, in due time after he was gone, proper receipts and discharges were found from all persons, whether tradesmen or others, with whom he had any manner of trans- actions or money concerns. Mrs. HOWE, after the death of her children, thought proper to lessen her family of servants, and the expenses of her housekeeping; and therefore removed from her house in Jermyn-street to a little house in Brewer-street, near Golden-square. Just over against her lived one SALT *, a corn- chandler. About ten years after Howe's abdication, he contrived to make an ac- quaintance with Salt, and was at length in such a degree of intimacy with him, that he usually dined with Salt once or

---

* I knew SALT, whom I often met at a coffee- house called King's Coffee-house, near Golden- square. He related to me the particulars which I have here mentioned, and many others, which have escaped my memory.

twice a week. From the room in which they eat, it was not difficult to look into Mrs. Howe's dining-room, where she generally sate and received her company; and Salt, who believed Howe to be a bachelor, frequently recommended his own wife to him as a suitable match. During the last seven years of this gentleman's absence, he went every Sunday to St. James's church, and used to sit in Mr. Salt's seat, where he had a view of his wife, but could not easily be seen by her. After he returned home, he never would confess, even to his most intimate friends, what was the real cause of such a singular conduct; apparently, there was none: but whatever it was, he was certainly ashamed to own it. Dr. Rose has often said to me, that he believed

his brother HOWE* would never have returned to his wife, if the money which
he took with him, which was supposed to
have been 1000*l.* or 2000*l.* had not been
all spent: and he must have been a good
economist, and frugal in his manner of
living, otherwise his money would scarce
have held out; for I imagine he had his
whole fortune by him, I mean what he
carried away with him in money or bank
bills; and daily took out of his bag, like
the Spaniard in GIL BLAS, what was
sufficient for his expenses.

REVERENDO DE GREGE PORCUM is an
expression used by Dr. JOHN BURTON,

---

* And yet I have seen him after his return addressing his wife in the language of a young bridegroom.
And I have been assured by some of his most intimate
friends, that he treated her during the rest of their
lives with the greatest kindness and affection.

speaking of himself in a thing which he calls his ITER SUSSEXIENSE. This is borrowed, as we all know, from the EPICURI DE GREGE PORCUM of HORACE, which has been censured by some critics as a coarse expression, and not agreeable to the usual politeness of the Roman poet; but it certainly ought to be censured with some severity, as applied by this reverend divine to himself and the whole body of the clergy; for how are we to translate it,—one of the *reverend herd of swine?* or, in a more limited manner, *one of those clergymen who are hogs?* This is such an indecent, or rather such an infamous appellation, that I scarce believe the most fiery sectarist among us, or the greatest enemy to prelacy and the Church of England, would dare to throw out; and there

was a time when an author would have
been degraded and expelled the order
on which he had cast such an injurious
reflection. It is no alleviation of this
man's fault that he treats himself with
the same freedom with which he treats
his brethren : he best knows his own in-
clinations and the qualities both of his
body and mind; and whether they are
properly designed by this metaphorical
expression, which he has adopted from
the Roman satirist, he is certainly the
best judge. But may we not, therefore,
without offence, or the breach of good
manners, give him the name which he
himself has assumed? and when he is
instructing and admonishing the university (for all his sermons are in that strain),
would it be any impropriety to judge him
out of his own mouth, and apply to him

the old adage, sus Minervam? With an head full of Latin and Greek, Burton uses both these languages with as little taste and judgment as a school-boy.

Although I have been often prevailed on to write* a Latin epitaph, and have adhered, according to the best of my knowledge or information, to the truth in these panegyrical characters (for *de mortuis nil nisi bonum*, however it may be condemned in history, has been an allowed maxim in all monumental

---

* I promised Nash, a few years before he died, that if I survived him, I would write his epitaph. I performed my promise, and in my description of this extraordinary phenomenon, I think I have written nothing but the truth; one thing I omitted, which I did not reflect on until after the epitaph was printed, that a statue had been erected to him whilst he was living; and this great honour had been conferred on him with more justice than to any other of his contemporaries or brother kings.

inscriptions in these latter ages); yet this is a task which I have always very unwillingly undertaken. I could wish we had not departed from the simplicity of the old Roman inscriptions; for as our modern epitaphs consist generally of a string of fulsome praises, bestowed equally on the best and the worst, so they are generally disregarded, and if they are ever read, are read for the sake of the composition only. The dean and prebendaries of Westminster sell the sacred ground to any persons who think proper to purchase it; no objection is made to the quality or character of those to whom a monument is to be erected under this holy roof: the peer and the player, the chaste and the unchaste, are here deposited without distinction. But if you examine their characters, as those are

here engraven on the monumental marble, you will not find one person amongst
them all, who, when living, had not been
endowed with the most eminent qualities
both of body and mind. General ————
who rose to his high post by such arts as
are a disgrace to human nature, appears
in Westminster Abbey to have possessed
as great talents and as many virtues as
Scipio Africanus. I have been often
very undeservedly abused, and crimes
have been imputed to me, which, I thank
God, my honest soul abhors: on the
other hand, such praises have been frequently bestowed on me as I am conscious to myself I do not merit; and I
have on many occasions received an applause to which, I think, I was not entitled. *Laudatur ab his, culpatur ab illis,*
will probably be my fate during my life:

however, I would willingly, if I had
power, after my death, prevent the eulo-
gies of my friends, as well as the outrage
of my enemies; and therefore I offer
both to one and the other the following
epitaph or inscription :

Fui
Guilielmus King, LL. D.
. Ab anno MDCCXIX ad annum MDCCLX
Aulæ B. M. V. in Academiâ Oxon. Præfectus.
Literis humanioribus à puero deditus,
Eas usque ad supremum vitæ diem colui.
Neque vitiis carui, neque virtutibus,
Imprudens et improvidus, comis et benevolus;
Sæpè æquo iracundior,
Haud unquam, ut essem implacabilis.
A luxuriâ pariter ac avaritiâ
(Quam non tam vitium,
Quam mentis insanitatem esse duxi)
Prorsus abhorrens,
Cives, hospites, peregrinos
Omnino liberaliter accepi;
Ipse et cibi abstinentior, et vini abstinentissimus.
Cum magnis vixi, cum plebeiis, cum omnibus,
Ut homines noscerem, ut meipsum imprimis :

Neque, eheu, novi!
Permultos habui amicos,
At veros, stabiles, gratos
(Quæ fortasse est gentis culpa)
Perpaucissimos.
Plures habui inimicos,
Sed invidos, sed improbos, sed inhumanos :
Quorum nullis tamen injuriis
Perinde commotus fui,
Quàm deliquiis meis.
Summam, quam adeptus sum, senectutem
Neque optavi, neque accusavi,
Vitæ incommoda neque immoderatè ferens,
Neque commodis nimiùm contentus:
Mortem neque contempsi,
Neque metui.

DEUS OPTIME,
Qui hunc orbem et humanas res curas,
Miserere animæ meæ!

THE END.

LONDON :

PRINTED BY T. DAVISON, WHITEFRIARS.

CPSIA information can be obtained
at www.ICGtesting.com
Printed in the USA
BVHW09*1333160818
524721BV00016B/1413/P